An Eye For Joy

NOTICING THE GOOD WORLD EVERYWHERE

PEG GUILFOYLE

Sea Crow Press

*All that I hope to say in books, all that I ever hope to say,
is that I love the world.*

— E.B. White

*This book is dedicated to my readers,
whose kind attention and wise eyes keep me upright
and hopeful.*

Contents

NOTICING, WONDER, AND JOY

This is a book about the impulse to wonder, the practice of noticing, and the inclination toward joy.

When my children were small and we gathered at the dinner table, I often made a little maternal speech. "Tell me one thing," I would say, "that you saw or heard or thought or learned today that was beautiful or funny or interesting or new." It was a way of talking, yes (and getting them to talk), but I also wanted them to learn a kind of perception. I wanted the beautiful or funny or interesting or new things to pop out from the background, surrounded by a little glow, a little buzz, and lodge themselves in their consciousness. I didn't want them to miss the wondrous details enmeshed in the quotidian.

I don't want to miss them either. So, often—sometimes multiple times a day —I make the same speech to the universe on my own behalf: *Come on, universe; show me one thing.*

The more I ask, the more it shows me.

It will show you too.

What might you see? Joy, surprise, wonder, everyday beauty, everyday sustenance, and hope. Faith in humanity in all its wild diversity and clamor.

Each day is a box with a surprise inside.

I was in New York for a few days not long ago. It happened to be Fleet Week, when the maritime services bring thousands of sailors to the city. They were exuberant and joyful on the street. I watched the parade of ships up the Hudson, where fireboats waited to escort them and to rearrange a portion of the river into the sky.

A fellow in cargo shirts and a cap told me the ships always pause at the 9/11 Memorial where white-clad sailors salute from their decks. "It is always," he said quietly, looking out over the water, "a dramatic moment."

There is also something called Snag Yourself a Sailor during Fleet Week, an idea that provided me with a constant smile, watching the fit and beautiful sailors in their dress whites make their way through the crowds, heads turning at their progress.

Dragging my rolling bag up the steps at the Metropolitan Museum of Art, I was stopped by a guard who sadly explained that the cloakroom would not let me check my suitcase. Then she confided, *sotto voce*, that the hot dog truck—she pointed to the street—was a good alternative. The vendor would store my bag for the afternoon for $10.

And indeed he did, shoving it under the hot-dog grill. "Been doing this for seventeen years," he said, smiling. "Go see some art." He waved me on to the Cycladic Art exhibit and the Costume Institute. Made good hot dogs too.

Later that day, on a crowded subway platform, I asked a stolid man: "What do you think, is this the right way into the city?" Then I noticed his T-shirt graphic: *I crave solitude. Don't talk to me.* He did not smile, but he did point at a nearby overhead sign with the word *Manhattan* and a large, red arrow. I nodded my thanks and turned away.

Back in the Midwest a few days later, I biked through a lovely little pocket park, nestled at the foot of the High Bridge in St. Paul. I was having a thoughtful day and stopped to settle on a stone bench. Something caught my attention. Behind an iron gate, the ground growth had gone to luxuriant weeds. Up through the weeds were two pale, pink poppies—lovely, fragile, and indomitable. Making their way up through the spiky underbrush to offer passersby a moment of beauty.

Poppies self-sow. When we are alert, human beings tend to do the same with beauty, splendor, and awe: one small sighting leads to another. One's eye sharpens for the lovely, even when it springs from the weeds. Soon you notice it everywhere.

As the master essayist E.B. White wrote: "Always be on the lookout for the presence of wonder."

It can be anywhere. Some years ago, not knowing why, I brought home an old printer's slug, which caught my eye in a dusty antique shop. The image had probably been a header for a newspaper column in the 1930s or '40s. It shows a woman sitting at her desk, typewriter before her, trash can below to receive rejected drafts. Above the desk, in the space between her head and her hands, floats a large question mark.

She is leaning in, abstracted, curious, alert—ready to notice—susceptible to a spark, available to ignite.

Often I feel the image is of me. Perhaps it is of you too.

Joy is everywhere. Our difficult world is also a good world, full of humanity and kindness. Joy is around every corner, lifting our spirits and providing illumination to the dark.

We all have the capacity to notice the good world and to bend ourselves toward joy, in both small and profound ways. Glimpses of the big. Every day. Everywhere. With everyone.

PART ONE

Noticing the Good World in Art

ONE

The Broncho Buster

I have a theory that a person who travels a lot, as I do, who is away from home base a good deal of the time, has to develop protective habits, ongoing interests that provide a certain sense of continuity, when any given month may find you in Tucson or Chicago or, say, Denver. These interests should have several common characteristics—they should have variety within a theme, they should be rooted in whatever locale you are in, they should give you an excuse to talk to interesting people along the way. They should, above all, be portable. (Wasn't there a television correspondent who did paintings of hotel lamps?)

My protective coloration of late has led me into a rather obscure, or at least out-of-fashion, branch of the fine arts. I'm getting interested in public statuary, those great bronze or stone monoliths that decorate parks and plazas and public buildings all across the country. You know. You've seen them. The big things featured on postcards with a building in the background? They seem to have been there forever, overlooked in a way because of their very permanence. You ignore them, your parents ignored them, your grandparents may have ignored them too. Only the pigeons seem to pay close attention, and they are notoriously indiscriminate in choice of company.

There is some beautiful public sculpture in Denver. I like to think that I would have stood and applauded at the unveiling, for example, of *The Broncho Buster*, the huge bucking horse with a masterful cowboy astride it, that stands downtown in Civic Center Park. All that bronze is poised midair over two firmly planted forelegs. The rider is waving his arm for balance and, we suspect, for a little flair besides.

The Broncho Buster was unveiled in 1918, and it is a direct and immediate throwback to the time when a bucking horse and cowboy could frequently be seen on the city's streets and Wild West Denver was largely corrals and longhorns. The statue was modeled from life. Sculptor Alexander Phimister Proctor carefully selected both horse and rider. The cowboy was a 6-foot-3 fellow named Red from Pendleton, Oregon. In his autobiography, Proctor says, "If anyone gave him five dollars and a drink of whiskey, [Red] would ride one of the buffaloes. The Cayuse [the horse, gentle readers] was a walleyed brute, a direct offspring of the devil." Proctor was a kind of participatory sculptor, an "animalier" as the French called sculptors and painters who worked with animals. He often used large creatures as subjects for his sculptures. He was once sketching intently while close to the bars of a panther's cage and turned his back to get better light on the drawing. "Suddenly," he says, "I felt needle-sharp points in my shoulder. Leaping away from the cage, I turned to see the big male cat's foreleg—at least six feet long, it looked to be—stretched through the cage, my blood dripping from his claws. Then and there I learned an important lesson for an artist: never turn your back on a wild four-legged model!"

Proctor was, in fact, not one for turning his back on much of anything. He was born in Ontario in 1862 and traveled as a child from his country into this country by covered wagon. He grew up in Denver with two ambitions: to succeed as an artist and to become a great hunter. As a boy, the two were not always in concert—he didn't like his first art lessons because they interfered with baseball and rabbit hunting. The Proctor family spent summers in Grand Lake, traveling there in the covered wagon and living a rough outdoor life that delighted the boy. When he was sixteen, Proctor killed an elk and his first grizzly in a single day of hunting. The adult Proctor believed that an artist's work must reflect the life that he lives, and all his life he would return again and again to the West, hunting, fishing, trapping, living among cowboys and Native Americans and using many of them as models. Eventually, he would bring his wife and all seven children along on those expeditions.

He studied, of course, in Paris and New York, and undertook many famous commissions, including sculpting the wonderful animals and décor for the elephant, lion, and primate houses at the Bronx Zoo. The mounted Native American figure called *On the War Trail*, which stands opposite *The Broncho Buster,* is also by Proctor. Together, the bronzes are heroic in concept, let alone in execution.

For his work on that fiery Cayuse broncho you hardly glance at while fighting traffic on Colfax, Proctor described a modeling session:

"One day when Red brought him into the studio to pose, he nearly kicked my hat off my head with his left hindfoot without seeming to move a muscle. Then began a scene that can be imagined better than described. The studio was only fourteen by sixteen, just large enough for a horse and two men if everyone was quiet. With a kicking and bucking horse, there was only room for the horse and one man, and that wasn't me. I had sometimes had trouble in close quarters with wild animals but had always managed to save myself and my model. That time all I wanted to save was my hide. Stovepipe, splinters, boxes, table, and high profanity flew around for a time until Red finally got the beast settled down."

That work from life was done in Pendleton, Oregon, 1915. Red, incidentally, was later convicted of horse stealing.

TWO

Art at the Airport

"We should all do, in the long run, what gives us joy," says the essay master E.B. White. With the freedom of an essayist, I am in leisurely contemplation today of the differences between a focused mind and a mind willing to wander, and the relationship of both to environment. My field of study is the Minneapolis–St. Paul International Airport, where the human tendency is toward purposeful, with a dash of harried. Got your bag? Your ID? Your offspring? Better focus!

There is another possibility. At our airport these days we can enjoy the sight of a large-scale abstract sculpture, or the color and sweep of a mosaic representing the Mississippi. Perhaps a different mindset is in order. Something like the difference between narrow and wide aperture? Or just the elasticity of time in which one moment you are rushing toward your journey and the next you're sitting on that bench on the other side of security, glancing at your timepiece, which is, for the moment, on your side. Put that phone down and see your surroundings as something other than an impediment to making that plane. Now you can afford to look around.

Astute planners at our airport are thinking beyond that basic dissonance and bridging it on our behalf. They are making a complex process work. Bravo!

Hurrah for the arts program at MSP airport, and its desire for your eye. Ben Owen, director of Arts@MSP, calls its intention "surprise and delight". Artist Kipp Kobayashi calls it "momentary respite". Alan Howell, senior architect for the Metropolitan Airports Commission, says, "We put art in the spaces where people are."

Owen, an art appreciator, master organizer, and expert networker, says his mission is to transform space to place. Aspects of the work: Conceive and install public artworks in an unartistic built environment for viewers who might not be in the mood to enjoy art; Include long-term installations and rotating exhibits; Make the art nongeneric and place-oriented; Choose work that allows interaction; Display art in the terminals and on the concourses, on the parking ramps and in the restrooms. Overhead, underfoot. Lit and lively, and anchored by a signature piece that pierces both the departure and arrival levels, reminding us with shape and light that leaving and returning are part of the same journey. You are flying out of your home airport, and you will return home at travel's end.

Lift up your eyes from your wheelie. Here are a few highlights, from this member of the traveling public.

The aforementioned signature piece, called *The Aurora*, with tech-responsive lake shapes embedded in the floor below. Yes, that is Lake Phalen among them, and yes, you can jump on the lake. The colors above you change when you wave your arms at the "sky."

Watch for many floor and wall mosaics and a significant number of installations near the restrooms. "Put art in the spaces where people are." Take a look at restrooms on the retail mall and at Gates C6 and F10.

Seek out the gallery in Concourse C, where the airport's electric carts used to be lined up to recharge. Now it's a rotating delight. Notice that many of the artists are local. Consider what a commission like this means to the artists, who are our neighbors. Think about reach. Forty million people pass through MSP every year.

And note especially Steve Ozone's *Interrupted Landscapes of the Incomer*, nearly 400 feet long, installed on the side of the Silver Parking Ramp, seen cinematically from the moving walkway between Concourses C and G. Ben Owen remembers that an Ozone installation was discussed at his very first staff meeting, and the conversation was tending toward large-scale flowers.

"I asked him [Ozone] to consider something more representational and meaningful," Owens said. "I went to his studio and saw some of these portraits, which are of people who live in Northeast Minneapolis. People who came from elsewhere and chose Minnesota as their home." In short, incomers.

Ozone's work here was inspired by his own family's experience; his grandfather came to the United States from Japan in 1906. The MSP portraits are enormous and compelling, showing immigrants from Kenya, Syria, Mexico, Japan, Yugoslavia, Poland . . . and Jacksonville, Florida. Installed on pierced steel panels that somehow evoke pointillism, they are in more than heroic scale. At almost 16,000 square feet, the Ozone piece is the largest mural in Minnesota.

These artworks have sometimes been unveiled without fanfare (opening events have been postponed for some sixteen pieces installed during the pandemic, and identifying placards are yet to come), and yet they excel every day at their primary work. Catching the eye. Prompting a smile. Causing a pause. Lifting the gaze. Lodging in your perception. Perhaps even opening the heart. Just as public artworks ought to do.

THREE

Minnesota in Chicago

In Chicago this winter, I spent a solitary day at the Art Institute, wandering happily among many things I love. The Impressionists! *A Sunday on La Grande Jatte—1884!* The Greek and Roman galleries! Arms and armor! The Thorne Rooms! All worthy of exclamation points.

This visit, I re-sorted my time a little, accessing the collections list and using keyword *Minnesota* to see what turned up. Many wonderful things did: photographer Gordon Parks, architect Frank Gehry's concept sketch of the Weisman Art Museum, the work of potter Warren MacKenzie.

There are sixty-six artworks on that list. All but one are in storage; I imagine a long, climate-controlled shelf with the sixty-five pieces and a small arrow marked "Minnesota." Could there be just one available to see? The curator helping me checked my methodology by using another state name as a search term; *New York* turned up 4,135 artworks.

I poked the curator a little. "What," I said, "is the Institute thinking? So many related to New York and so few related to Minnesota." He smiled and gave me directions.

The Minnesota piece on view is in a grand location in the huge atrium that surrounds and encompasses the Woman's Staircase. Its official name is *Teller's wicket from the National Farmers Bank, Owatonna, Minnesota, 1906/08.* The wicket and the bank are the work of famous architect Louis

Sullivan, who strongly influenced Frank Lloyd Wright and the Prairie School style of architecture.

A wicket, I learned, is "a service window where a customer conducts trans-actions with a teller." Hence the bottom slot, where paper and money could be presented or received. And, I suppose, hence the beautiful oval framing which makes it easy to picture a smiling teller, probably a hand-some young man in a starched collar. "Hello," he would say. "How may I help you today?"

In the Owatonna bank, the farmers bank, I think it likely that the teller would have known most of his customers, so let's make it "Hello, Mr. Nill-son. How may I help you today?"

The wicket is made of copper-plated cast iron, curlicued and elaborate with hardly a straight line in it. The curators at the Minneapolis Institute of Art (which, curiously, possesses a 1967 cast of the one in Chicago) describe it as "overlaid with scrolling curves and organic designs of pods, leaves, and berries...meant to be seen and appreciated at close range." So, I'll bet, was the face of a young smiling man in the teller cage, framed in that ornate oval.

The Chicago wicket was given by the manufacturer to the Art Institute of Chicago in 1908. Seven others were mounted in the bank and removed during renovations in 1929 and 1940. None of them has survived; if the prescient manufacturer had not made its gift to Chicago, the ornamenta-tion work of Scottish-born George Grant Elmslie would exist only in dim photographs.

Chicago credits Louis Sullivan as the artist, and the Elmslie name does not appear. MIA credits Elmslie as the designer, noting that Sullivan designed the building. Elmslie was Sullivan's chief draftsman and ornamental designer, at one time sharing an office with Frank Lloyd Wright. Prairie School architect Elmslie was part of the team that designed the Purcell-Cutts House in Minneapolis; he maintained partnerships and an office in Minneapolis from 1909 to 1921.

I like to think of these fertile minds, the Prairie School minds, intersecting with one another over their lifetimes in the Midwest and leaving us with buildings, ornaments, beauty that still strike the eye with pleasure. Two or three of them together, collaborating, quarreling, reuniting in a fluid interaction of ideas, the manifestation of which is still available to our Midwestern eyes.

In the later part of his career, Louis Sullivan and his associates, including Elmslie, took commissions for a series of smaller bank and commercial buildings in the Midwest; the Owatonna National Farmers' Bank is one of them. Between 1908 and 1920, he designed nine; they are sometimes called Sullivan's Jewel Boxes. All still stand. Many have remarkable Prairie School details extant, including a massive stained-glass arch window in Owatonna.

Owatonna is sixty-nine miles from St. Paul. It would make an excellent road trip. See the wicket in Chicago or Minneapolis beforehand. Other possible stops on a Prairie School exploration: the Purcell-Cutts House in Minneapolis; the Harold C. Bradley House in Madison, Wisconsin; Taliesin in Spring Green, Wisconsin, resting your eye on surviving traces of a time when those new ideas influenced the built world of the Midwest, and left beauty for us to enjoy all these years later.

FOUR

Outside a Stage Door: Orbach's 42nd Street

Some years ago, when I was a hotshot stage manager, I considered moving to New York to work on Broadway. I knew people there, and I settled for three weeks in a friend's empty apartment on the Upper East Side and started calling and wandering around. I was invited to see shows. I was invited to watch from backstage. And I spent considerable time near the stage doors, watching the companies go in and out, and trying to get a sense of what working life was like on, yes, the Great White Way. It looked, I must say, pretty hard-bitten.

If you wanted to be swept away by the romance of Broadway, there was no better show to see than *42nd Street*, the stage chock-full of giggling chorus girls and boys and pounding tap shoes, lit by garish neon and the loving representation of every Broadway trope, right down to getting off the bus from Allentown and becoming a star. In a sense, I was thinking about getting off the bus myself.

I watched from out front, rapt. Went out under the white-lit marquee at the intermission to be part of the street scene. Rose to my feet with everyone else when Jerry Orbach, all magnetism and power as the Big Producer Julian Marsh, led the entire company into the signature song. "Hear the beat of dancing feet," he trumpeted. "It's the song I love the melody of . . . 42nd Street!" Then the tap shoes took over.

(Yes, you know Jerry Orbach. The original company of *The Fantasticks*. The original Billy Flynn in *Chicago*. And twelve years as Detective Lennie Briscoe on television's *Law and Order*. What a presence!)

After the show, I came out with the crowd, walking slowly away and across the boulevard in a backdrop of real-world traffic, horns, lights, bright buildings. The theater was, I seem to recall, very close to the actual 42nd Street. I heard a familiar voice behind me calling out "Taxi!" and turned in time to see Mr. Orbach, arm still raised, rushing toward a taxi swerving toward the curb. He ducked in—he was tall—and was rushed away. And I thought . . . well, that was the real working life: spotlights and tumultuous applause, then quickly out of costume, out the stage door, and hailing a taxi. I still think of it as a distillation of everything New York, along with eating leftover Chinese food for breakfast, and chatting up the bag man at Grand Central. A working stiff taxi driver was hailed by a Broadway star. Cab and star zoomed away into the bright night traffic. Could there be anything more New York than that?

FIVE

Inside a Stage Door: Burton's Camelot

As a young stage manager exploring New York, I would call the theaters and get the production stage managers on the phone, explaining that I had credentials and was thinking about relocating to the city. Could I shadow them? A surprising number said yes. I hope I thanked them proportionately to the favor.

That is how I found myself watching the Richard Burton *Camelot* from backstage at Lincoln Center.

There was, and is, a certain kind of geography in the wings; a person who knows how to be still can just about tuck up near the stage manager, who often runs the show from the stage right downstage corner. You are very close but out of the sightlines. All the concentration is onstage. To get there, each performer must cross between the dark and the light, a single step that contains all the magic and power and propulsion of the theater. It happens thousands of times every week in the theater world, but no audience member has ever seen it. No audience member ever will. Offstage is the mechanism of the theater, with prop tables and dirt and costume racks and stagehands lounging around the fly rail, waiting to pull scenery. Onstage is the magic.

In the wings at *Camelot*, I was enthralled, watching the mechanism work and listening to the story unfold onstage. Merlyn and Arthur and Guinevere. Then Lancelot. A familiar story, old and strong. Actors would appear from the downstairs dressing rooms, or disappear there. Toward the end of the first act, the chorus—Knights of the Round Table—appeared in very offstage mode, shuffling and clunking up the stairs, poking and whispering, indifferent, pedestrian. Burton as King Arthur was moving toward his speech at the end of the first act, when he is discovering that Guinevere does not love him.

From the script:

"I mean, when people hear . . . what has happened at Camelot . . . they may lay down their arms and come of their own free will . . . it's quite possible no one will bear arms at all anymore . . . and that there will really be peace . . . all borders will disappear . . . and all the things I dreamed . . . I dreamed . . . I dreamed . . . (His voice trails off in utter defeat, and he stands motionless in an abject trance. The sound of the March to the Grand Hall is heard in the orchestra, as the lights dim slowly.)"

When that sound was heard from the orchestra pit, the ragged line of actors offstage began to straighten. Several crushed out their surreptitious cigarettes. They filed past the prop table, picking up their spears. As they crossed into the light, they set their jaws and transformed each by each into someone entirely else. Sir Someone. And Sir Someone Else.

Years have passed since that moment in New York, and I have had trouble placing the moment when Burton was declaiming onstage in his deep, round tones, and the chorus men were preparing to march on. So I called Tony Vierling, the Twin Cities musical theater actor who has done three Camelots. Tony found that moment in his no-doubt-battered script and refreshed me on the counterpoint of the onstage oratory and the chorus men.

"I found it!" he said. "This is it! Exactly the moment! So powerful, he is willing to sacrifice his love for them both for this great ideal. And so tragic. Then this beautiful moment of pomp, ceremony, and tradition. This is the exact moment! Whew!"

Tony, who lives a life full of exclamation points, has spent decades stepping across that threshold from the dark into the light. He knows the moment of change well, and the moment of power too.

I decided against pursuing New York and came back to the Midwest to spend my life, this life, here. I've watched many fine performers cross that line from the dark into the light, dropping their own personae to the deck as they step through, assuming something beyond themselves in the same way the chorus boys dropped their cigarettes, grasped their spears, threw their shoulders back, and became noble.

"The Knights of the Court," says the script, "parade to the Grand Hall with banners flying in ceremonial drill." And so they did, and Burton made his exit, and I watched them go.

SIX

From the Golden Age of Scenic Art

The Elitch Theatre, Denver's grand old lady of summer stock, where I was fortunate to once work as stage manager, required a few unique aspects to my preshow routines. It also had one gloriously unique piece of house scenery.

First the customary routines, familiar to all backstage folk. Getting into your blacks to promote invisibility. Checking the call sheets to ensure the actors are all in the house. Knocking at each dressing room door to check temperature and climate of the company and the leading celebrity. The time-honored calls—first the half-hour and then the 15. Prop tables set, scenery in place for the top.

Working with front of house to open the doors, while hearing the muttering of the audiences who were, in this theater, generally big and happy. Checking in with the crew heads, props, carpenters, and electricians, particularly the flymen and the often-beleaguered wardrobe man and dresser. Checking the sightlines and masking, so the secrets of the backstage could remain so. I always liked to put a hand on the grand drape—red velvet, heavily weighted at the bottom—and look upward to the distant grid, still on the same hemp rope system installed in 1890.

Quick look at the prompt script; leave it open to the top. Test the cue lights and headsets. Before the five, work lights out and pre-set up, at which point the dimness and the cavernous backstage could begin to work their magic.

Take my place at the calling position, where 100 years of predecessors had also stood, stage right downstage near the fly rail, the center of it all.

The un-customary, unique-to-Elitch's: the auditorium was cooled by a set of overhead fans, making a steady whirring sound on hot summer nights. Woe (I say, woe!) to the stage manager who neglected to turn those off before the curtain went up and the actors began to speak. Do not spoil those star entrances!

And then, at the five-minute call, a moment particular to this house.

In the farthest downstage position, closest to the audience, Elitch's had a house curtain from the golden age of American scenic art. Hand-painted by brush and stencil in 1894 by the Charles Thompson Scenic Studio of Los Angeles, rich in color and complex in decoration, the curtain's central image was an English-style cottage-in-a-garden, with a cartouche that declared, ungrammatically but charmingly, "Anne Hathaway's cottage, a mile away, Shakespeare sought, at close of day." Hence, dubbed the "Annie."

At the five-minute call, the stagehands, with care and a touch of ceremony, flew the old curtain up and out of sight, revealing the deep folds of the grand drape, the last thing left between the actors and the audience. When it, too, flew, the house lights went down, the stage was revealed, and the play began. Far above that noise and glamor and sound, the glorious Annie, like a huge painting, would hang silently in the dark of the fly loft, always there and always ready.

Research tells a little. In 1890 Elitch's had been built with 600 seats and a canvas roof "at the end of a winding path through the apple orchard." There are references that the earliest audiences could stand in the gardens and still hear the play. The original curtain, featuring scenes of the Rocky Mountains and the surrounding gardens, would have had exposure to the weather. Was it rained on and ruined? Windblown and torn? This is specu-lation, informed speculation. In any event, after only four years, it was replaced with the Annie.

Why did the theater's leadership commission a house curtain with a painting of distant Stratford-upon-Avon? The house at the time was offering six weeks of light opera with four weeks of vaudeville, "suitable family entertainment of the type wholly acceptable to women and children." Why make the dominant image, the first thing the audience would see, refer to the Bard?

I've read that Shakespeare and his works were as well-known in the United States in the 19th century as they are today. In his great 1835 book *Democracy in America*, Alexis de Tocqueville remarked on Shakespeare's popularity in this country, writing, "There is hardly a pioneer's hut that does not contain a few odd volumes of Shakespeare. I remember that I read the feudal drama of *Henry V* for the first time in a log cabin."

Now there's an image. "Can this cockpit hold the vasty fields of France?" *Henry V* read by the traveling Frenchman in a log cabin in distant America.

As historian Lawrence Levine has written, Shakespeare was widely performed on professional stages at the same time that he was playfully lampooned in parodies and minstrel shows that depended for their humor on a wide knowledge of his work. Shakespeare, in short, said *American Theatre* magazine, was America's most popular playwright, and part of the lore was his older sweetheart Anne Hathaway, who grew up in a pretty village near Stratford.

For 19th-century actors, as for those in our time, Shakespeare was regarded as a kind of epitome of the art and craft. If you were a Shakespearean, that meant a certain level of skill and depth. So too for theatrical companies and, we can deduce, for growing, ambitious Elitch's. Playmakers and playgoers alike might have been struck and caught by the imagery of rural England and Shakespeare.

By 1897 the widow Mary Elitch had a resident stock company in Denver with a full season of plays featuring actors from both coasts. In the 1900 season, she presented *As You Like It* as the first play by Shakespeare on the Elitch stage, part of a full season of sixteen productions. Shakespeare had arrived at Elitch's, and that first audience was greeted by the sight of the Anne Hathaway curtain.

When Mary Elitch and her fellows considered a design for the new curtain for their theater, they were likely shown a display book of curtain images to choose from, where they saw the image of Anne Hathaway's rustic cottage.

"This one," they might have said. "Let's have this one." But how did that image get into that display book?

Research can be a joy.

Wilfrid Williams Ball (1853–1917) was a British Victorian and Edwardian who made a series of artworks on a trip from London to Stratford-upon-Avon in the early 1880s. Shakespearean tourism was quite a thing in that period, as it is now. His watercolor of Anne Hathaway's cottage somehow made its way to the display book in Los Angeles, and thence to the playhouse curtain in Denver. Versions of his Annie image can be found on eBay to this day.

Emily White of the Shakespeare Birthplace Trust in Stratford, which manages the cottage, supplies a clue:

"Anne Hathaway's Cottage became symbolic of England, and was used by numerous companies to sell their products. That particular view of the cottage was, by far, the most favored by artists. It is also the view which visitors saw when walking from the center of Stratford upon Avon to the hamlet of Shottery to view the cottage. By the 1880s, it was a standard part of the visitor experience to walk the mile from Stratford, using the same historic path that Shakespeare once likely walked."

It is a pleasant reconstruction to think that Mr. Ball's work was seized upon by the scenic studio as an attractive theatrical image, and was chosen by the representatives of the grand Denver playhouse for their new curtain. It is not pleasant to recount that in interim years, after the closing, when the playhouse was still standing but before restoration, its roof leaked. The Annie was first damaged, then terribly damaged, then taken down and folded up in a dressing room. The building is still standing, survived—and bravo to that—but when the Annie was unrolled on the stage floor, six years later, only paint flakes and dust were left.

The Annie is lost now; we are fortunate that the theater itself has been saved. Old theaters, and new ones, traditionally leave a single light burning on an empty stage, the last thing lit before the doors are locked at night. It doesn't reach into all the dim corners or up high above where the Annie once flew. But it can serve as a gathering place for the spirits and history and energy that fills these old houses, which is why they are traditionally called "ghostlights." A ghostlight still burns on the old stage at Elitch's; perhaps a ghostly echo of the beautiful Annie hangs in the dark above.

SEVEN

No Blue-Sky Thinking

"We pledge to fight 'blue-sky thinking'
wherever we find it.
Life would be dull if we had to look up
at cloudless monotony day after day."
(from the manifesto of the Cloud Appreciation Society)

I have been a sky-watcher all my life. Among other treasures on my grandparents' spine-faded bookshelves were the Scribner Classics, a series begun in 1904 and featuring many of the best illustrators of the 20th century. Some twenty-five volumes (*Treasure Island*, *The Last of the Mohicans*, *The Scottish Chiefs*, *The Boy's King Arthur*) featured the work of N.C. Wyeth with cover images and interior plates that carried me far away from that little house outside Chicago onto islands and into the primeval forest and the Scottish Highlands. Wyeth died five years before I was born, but his work shaped the way I look at the sky.

Illustrators and painters are storytellers as much as writers, and one of Wyeth's greatest atmospheric techniques was his work with clouds. His pirates and frontiersmen, knights and chieftains were nearly always framed by startling skies. When I settled into the big rocker in my grandparents' modest home, that luminous imagery leapt from the page, opening a passageway to Stirling Castle or Sherwood Forest. If the early 20th century prose now seems complex and even turgid, the stories are evergreen, and the paintings still rich and vital.

Passageway and escape route. There were considerably fewer towering land-scapes and less drama outside the pages of the books. The *plunk plunk plunk* of practicing piano, arithmetic with Sister Rosario, and fish sticks on Friday night did not match the soaring visions of my book-fed imagination. I was always looking at the world with the mind's eye. Perhaps you were too.

And I saw things in the clouds, as the children do in Wyeth's *The Giant*. Just like those little ones he created with their buckets and shovels, I spent much of my childhood on a beach gazing upward at the changeable mighty skyscape over Lake Michigan. Every moment, the world presented itself in clouds and drama and limitless change. Wyeth painted *The Giant*, I read, in memoriam for a student lost to tuberculosis. The original, 5 by 6 feet, has been hanging since 1923 in an East Coast boarding school dining room. The figure in the white hat represents the lost student; the others are meant to be Wyeth's own children.

Years later in Minnesota, I hung a far-smaller copy of that image for my children when they were old enough to start their own lives of sky-gazing. One hangs now in the shared room of my little granddaughters, who are the right age to find the cloud-shapes and the giant shape equally real. The girls still live in the liminal space between tangible and intangible, probable and improbable, on the beach in the wind.

Not long ago, I sought a conversation with a plein air painter who has worked for decades to transfer the limitless depths of clouds and sky to the little flat surface of the canvas, changing it to a world into which the viewer can step.

Mary Pettis, an expressive realist, says, "When I paint, I truly feel the great relations among all things. Every subject becomes a metaphor. I forget to breathe." Our conversation was rapid, packed, and fascinating. I too forgot to breathe.

A photo on Pettis's website expresses the joy she takes in her art. She is standing on a rocky shore with her working gear at hand: canvas, palette, and brushes. On her easel is her painting of water and sky. The foremost wave on her canvas is no longer present in the world; she caught it in its moment and recorded it. Mary says her paintings are like an aperture into the world, and although the rectangle of her canvas captures a kind of lens view, necessarily framed by its edges, her own vision extends beyond the canvas to encompass everything.

"I like to feel that every painting gives someone a sense that this world continues all the way around them," she says. "The same quality of light is coming out of the sky and landing everywhere, even though we see only its corners."

It seems to me this gives her work a kind of mystical extension into the place she was regarding with such close attention. What was the light? Where was the sun? How were the clouds moving? What were the colors needed to hold those clouds on her brush and then to release them onto the canvas?

With Mary Pettis's work, the conscious and unconscious response of the viewer are congruent. Our responses do not stumble over anything.

"Each cloud has its personality, but it's all connected, like walking through a crowd in Times Square," the painter told me. "We're bumping shoulders with other human beings. We look. We pause at the details or where there's a bright color or an interesting note.

"It's like a musical score. It gets quiet and then there's a little tinkle and then the sky has to be sympathetic to the painting. The sky and the clouds balance the view and help us stay in rhythm and harmony and not discord. When the color of the sky is in perfect sympathy with what's happening on the land, we feel at peace. We feel it's right."

And I'd venture that you might say the same thing about the function of sky and clouds in the real world. The feeling of peace, of "perfect sympathy" as she says, can occur when we're walking through the landscape. A good reason to look up.

Surrounded by her paintings in a gallery, I ask her, "Are you drawn to sunsets or sunrises or stormy skies or calm ones?"

"Yes," she answers, beaming. "Yes!"

I am an eight-year member of the Cloud Appreciation Society, and I am hardly alone. My membership number is 40,637. There is, almost certainly, a scholarly dissertation somewhere positing that the human desire to belong to a group is traceable back to our time huddling in caves and evading predators.

The Cloud Appreciation Society, based in Britain, publishes a cloud image every day direct to one's inbox. Members from all over the world send in their photos, tagged by location and with a few words describing the classification of that particular cloud. The effect is a daily tour of the atmosphere's vaporous beauties, and a reminder that all people everywhere stand under the same high sky. Lenticularis over Nerja, Spain. Towering cumulus over the Temple of Zeus, Greece. A turbulent storm system over central Singapore. Nacreous clouds over Elgin, Moray, Scotland. Cirrus over Cogdill Center, United States.

Sometimes the society's Cloud-A-Day is from a painting, which reminds us that the sky is infinitely interpret-able and style-able. David Hockney paints clouds differently than did Georgia O'Keeffe, who saw in a different way from Jim Denomie, whose paintings were entirely unlike those of Charles Russell. Or Mary Pettis. Or N.C. Wyeth.

When I visit an art museum, say the Minneapolis Institute of Art, with its relative silence, wealth of beauty, and rush of images, I sometimes employ a personal sorting mechanism, letting my eye glide around a gallery and catch on all the paintings with clouds. Then I step over and stand in front of each one and consider the infinite variety of our world and the infinite wonder of the artists' eye. And then I go outside to find a spot between the trees and look up.

Noticing the Good World in People

EIGHT

Elevator Sharing

Our apartment building is large and diverse, and I've become peculiarly fond of the elevator. Each ride holds the potential for a wonderful surprise. It provides the possible proximity to strangers, and I love strangers. When the door slid open today, a young worker boarded, pushing her cleaning cart. We both smiled. When I asked which floor she wanted and then added casually "How's it going?" the day changed.

She lit up like a torch, joy shooting out of her eyes. "I am going to have a baby! I just found out!" Already beautiful, she became exponentially more so, her startling joy filling the little box of the elevator car.

We had the length of that ride to enthuse together, to offer and receive congratulations, a particularly female connection. For me, it echoed my own motherhood; for both of us, the community of womanhood. An interaction of perhaps a minute; a pleasure still reverberating. She doubtless went on to tell her friends, her parents, her partner. But she told me too, and I am grateful. Can't wait to see her in the elevator again.

NINE

Girl Needs a Job

I was in a nearly empty small-town supermarket this summer and fell into a conversation with the checkout girl. I am always falling into conversations. It was a rather downscale grocery, and all the women workers were wearing drab smocks. This young lady was not yet twenty, I'd guess; she had disheveled hair, rather pale skin, and a bright grin. When she was packing my things, she smiled and said I should not worry. She would not squish my bread. I smiled back and said, thanks, I had every confidence, and that she was doing a good job of customer relations with me. She said that was good, because she was looking for work . . . and then our conversation took off.

What kind of work was she looking for? Anything that would give her forty hours. She didn't have that at the market? No, they gave her just enough hours so that she did not get benefits. Did she live locally? Yes, on a farm outside of town. I expressed my opinion that she would do well at whatever she chose. She confided that she had a job interview in a few days with a company that manufactures automotive brake components. It would be on Wednesday. I said that I'd be thinking of her on Wednesday and wishing her well.

She smiled and thought and paused and looked at me. She asked me a question that I found shattering.

Do you . . . work there? she asked me, and her face was bright with sudden hope and a touch of desperation.

For a minute, I think, she believed that I would turn out to be a recruiter, come into the store by chance. Her story would take a good turn. Her life would take a good turn.

I had to say no, and she absorbed that news without surprise or faltering. We parted as something like friendly strangers. And I did think of her on that Wednesday, and I'm thinking of her still, and I hope to heaven she got that job.

And I also hope that appreciation and encouragement from a friendly stranger, just that tiny amount, might have given her a boost, a bit of oomph, when she left the farm, and drove to that interview, having picked out clothes she thought would make the best impression.

Can you hear me, universe? Hire her. Hire her. And let it be a good job.

TEN

Run With The Enthusiasts

I am very partial to enthusiasts. It almost doesn't matter what their passions are. It's the ardor itself that sparkles and attracts. We are drawn to bright eyed enthusiasm, and some of the voltage, nearly discernible, rubs off on us. It's unmistakable, a two-way thing. We perceive it, are drawn to it, reflect it, and catch it. We are ignite-able.

An attorney of my acquaintance grew up in a musical family and is passionate about the violin. For years, he presented an annual private program, performing favorite chamber pieces and commenting with wit on the lives and dispositions of composers of the canon. Spellbinding, because he was an amateur in the truest sense, one who loves the subject.

Traveling in Las Vegas once, I wandered into the back of a body-building competition and watched the posing and the crowd, fascinated. An offstage builder smiled and said to me, "this is a very good family sport" and, at that moment, I was convinced. Enthusiasts can be found everywhere.

The operator of a vintage sawmill, who spent a summer day at a small-town Antique Power Show telling passers-by about the place of the sawmill in frontier history, and demonstrating over and over again. I brought home a piece of slag, an edge, rank with new wood smell.

A woman composer, magnetic by nature, who curates and introduces a classical music performance series, bouncing into view with an enormous smile saying "Hello! And welcome!"

I have a friend in the horse industry; her enthusiasms are the arcane details of breeding programs, the bright soft look of a new-born foal, and the consumption of evening champagne.

A planetary geologist I met at a Dark Sky Festival, who captivated deep winter audiences on a night when the far northern sky was completely obscured by clouds, and un-see-able. She was, she said, the Director of International Observe The Moon Night. An hour in her company, and you will long to depart this planet for elsewhere. She, no doubt, will be on board.

A plein-air painter who thrills to the impossible task of representing the ever-changing sky.

A young woman setting out on a fifty-day bike ride on the Pacific Coast Highway to raise awareness of suicide, having lost her veteran brother last year. She is fairly shining with health and eagerness, and mission. She wants to tell the story.

Enthusiasm is transmissible and, I would argue, life-giving. It is not the same as expertise, or charm, or even magnetism. It is different from the impulse to educate. It is, in a way, a child's capacity for engagement and wonder. It is a natural bubbler, as contagious as laughter, and the antipode of boredom in all its insidious manifestations. No yawn about it.

It's a gift that you have, and it's also a gift you can give. Love something, come alive with it, and then tell the world about it. There are nearly eight billion people on this planet. Your cohort is out there. Go find them. You'll have a lot to talk about.

Weary? Feeling a little grayed-out? Find an enthusiast, any subject, stand close enough to be caught, and start running.

ELEVEN

Meeting Sister Ebo

In 2015 I joined a Unitarian pilgrimage to Alabama for a symbolic march to commemorate the 50th anniversary of the voting rights march from Selma to Montgomery. Crossing the Edmund Pettus Bridge on March 7, 1965, hundreds of civil rights activists led by a young John Lewis were attacked and turned back by state and local police. That day became known as Bloody Sunday. Two days later Martin Luther King Jr. led a symbolic march to the bridge. Following a court ruling on the right to march, thousands gathered and crossed the bridge on March 21 and walked fifty-four miles in five days to reach the state capitol in Montgomery.

I hitched a ride from Montgomery to a memorial at Tabernacle Baptist in Selma to hear Dr. William Barber speak about poverty. At a Shiloh Baptist church supper, I listened to a Selma woman tell how her mother died untimely because the local hospital had no "Black blood" to give her. I made a friend of another marcher, a Black woman who looked over our group and said to me in confusion, "Who *are* you people? I didn't know there were any white people who cared about me and my family."

For me, the pilgrimage was a week about learning to be moved and sustained by the virtue of others and to feel joy in their presence. As I, exhausted, boarded the plane out of Birmingham, I encountered an unexpected and lasting blessing. I took my place and looked over at my seatmates. The little woman by the window was the justly famous civil rights activist Sister Antona Ebo, a nun who arrived in Selma in 1965 and was the only African American Catholic sister to march with Dr. King. Now she and a companion were flying home to St. Louis after crossing the bridge with President Obama and U.S. Representative John Lewis.

Sister Ebo had just been honored in the Legal Guardians Gallery of the National Voting Rights Museum and Institute in Selma. Nearing her ninety-second birthday, she was radiant, serene, unmistakably saintly, full of a vigorous joy, and very funny to boot.

When we arrived in Chicago, I was able to help Sister Ebo a little. We both had to change planes, and her connection was tight. I trotted ahead of the wheelchair, clearing people out of the way as we rushed to her gate. We made that wheelchair fly, laughing as we went; she called out an occasional "Have mercy!" When we parted, she said "The Lord had it on His agenda for us to meet today."

Although not my common parlance, all I could think was "Well then, thank you, Lord, thank you." And maybe, under my breath, "Have mercy."

TWELVE

Deciding for Dollars, Firsthand

I am a sucker for lemonade stands, one of my favorite forms of what might be called first hand philanthropy. No one steps up to a child-run stand for the beverage (Crystal Light powder, anyone?), but there are so many other good reasons.

Listening to a small-town outdoor concert last summer, I noted a child of perhaps ten years, with flyaway hair, going chair to chair with hand-drawn flyers for homemade lemonade only a block away.

She and her brother, just a touch older, were set up on the sidewalk with a pitcher, a bucket of ice, and a fine businesslike manner. I was the only customer in sight. "Two, please," I said, smiling.

"That will be four dollars, ma'am."

I lingered a minute to ask what they were raising money for, thinking camp or a bike or some special treat. "Oh," he said off-handedly, "just food. Our parents are both out of work right now. And last week, our dad was drunk and driving and had to spend the night in jail."

The girl piped up quickly, "They were wrong. He wasn't drunk. He was just tired from helping plan our lemonade stand and fell asleep while he was driving." Both children were just reporting the facts of their lives, their daily weather, their situation, in response to a friendly stranger. Just normal chit-chat.

Best lemonade I ever had, and the short stack of bills I left in their tip jar was the most satisfying donation I've made in years. It started me thinking about the extra gratification that comes with firsthand donations, a feeling that is not always present when you write that annual check to Something Big.

There is no doubt that our large giving systems and our big-name institutions have their place. There is work in the world that must be done on a large scale, and for that we need big systems and big buckets. I think, though, that giving can lose a little personality, a little jolt of connection, when we throw our relatively small drops into those big buckets. Direct relationship, even when momentary, reminds us that we are participants in a two-way transaction with our personal philanthropy. Recipients as well as givers. It flexes our capacity for empathy, raises our antennae for gratitude, and alerts us to everything we have in common with others. It encourages us to give again.

On that same summer journey, I attended an Antique Tractor and Power Show. I have a weakness for vintage machinery, loving to hear it sputter and roar, imagining how it once transformed the brawny American landscape from wild land to breadbasket. I was there far too early, and for an hour or two was the only visitor among fifty or sixty enthusiasts hooking up their sawmills and blades and farm machinery, coaxing them to life, then standing and admiring their noise and purposeful gyrations.

I was the first customer at the food tent, buying a plateful of biscuits and sausage gravy, ladled up from a row of crockpots by a fourteen-year-old member of the Future Farmers of America. I sat by the sawmill, chatting with the operator, and cadged a piece of slash, waste wood, to take home just because I liked the way it smelled. When it was too long to fit in my back seat, I was ushered over to a fellow selling used chain saws. My escort said, grinning, "Well, Steve over here has about fifty chain saws on his tables. Let's see if any of 'em work." The fourth one did.

As I left, I ambled by a plastic milk jug hung from a tree and labeled "Donations" in heavy black marker. I dropped in my five dollars. General nods of approbation from the members as I headed for the car, heavily scented now with fresh pine slash. I knew that my dollars were going toward something that I found wonderful. Isn't that one good way to sort our giving? Our sharing? Firsthand.

THIRTEEN

Thank You, Mrs. Z

My piano teacher, Iris Zahara, is gone. And I never told her what she'd meant to me.

It is a trope of middle age that one regrets not thanking the influential people in your life, and that regret proceeds from a mild ache to a kind of stabbing sensation when they depart. Somehow, I never cast back as far as my twelve-year-old self, living a suburban and limited life, walking weekly into the anteroom of a larger world, in which lived a beauty, and beauty itself. And now, in the classic and inevitable sense, Iris cannot hear me.

I think first about her hair, frequently roughed and rearranged by her restless hand. And the speed of her movements—unlike my mother and her club friends who seemed to flow through the air in a series of poses. Mothers leaned against the Chrysler while reaching into a flowery handbag. Poised attentively over the bridge table, studying their cards. Pausing at the parish to listen to Father O'Mara, heads slightly tilted and smiling.

Iris appeared to roar. Slim and tanned, she rushed through the church down the side aisle and arrived just in time at the organ seat, reaching out her feet for the flat slippers to play the pedals. She adjusted the stops. *Flick. Flick.* She twisted on the bench to look frankly, expectantly, unabashedly right at the altar; she lifted her long-fingered hands and when they came down, the church was filled with music. She favored complexity and ample use of the bass. Nothing timid. She liked long complicated runs on the keyboard or the foot pedals. She favored volume.

My first piano teacher was round Mrs. Salter, who called recitals "piano parties" and served cookies after. I'd started with her at a very young age, an earnest and biddable student. I liked to practice. The scales and repetitions didn't bore me. Sitting at the piano, I had my back turned to my life. It was a mechanical task that pleased my mother. My fingers were entirely under my control, and sometimes they made pleasing sounds. I practiced every day, focused entirely on the page and never looking at my hands, elbows stiff, with no intonation at all, and absolutely no pedal. *Plunk. Plunk. Plunk.*

There were no more cookies when I switched to Mrs. Zahara for lessons, and no more *plunk plunk plunk*. And what kind of name was Zahara anyway? Nothing Irish started with a Z.

Mrs. Z was a concert pianist, with a long, low-ceilinged studio overlooking her yard and creek. Two gleaming concert grand Steinways. Plenty of couches of the ultramodern variety—low and leather. Paintings, each illuminated by its own picture light on the walls between shelves and shelves of music. My time with Mrs. Z caused me to love cloudy afternoons. She would rush into the room to sit beside me on the bench. The music she gave me was exotic, dissonant, passionate, percussive, written by composers whose names I could not pronounce. It was not melodic. Because my brother would groan and complain as I approached the piano, finding a good time to practice became difficult.

Sometimes Mrs. Z would play for me to demonstrate something. Strong, strong attacks, plenty of dynamic control. Her hair would fly. Her arms were brown, her smile very white and very sudden. On the very best days, I would hear her playing through the open windows as I walked up the hill and glimpse her frowning in concentration over the keyboard. I would pause by the lilacs and look through the window at her, a woman working.

When my lesson was over, she would rush away. And I would pick up my music and walk home, abstracted, unsteady, my mind full of sound.

What did I learn in the studio, besides the *Khachaturian Toccata* and how to attack the keyboard? I learned that there was a life, not flat and repetitive, but based on beauty and music, a life of high standards and regular work to achieve them. It was an untethered life that included serious consideration of ideas and art, disagreement, discourse. There was a sense that life had the capacity for explosion. There were probably cocktail parties amid the Steinways, when interesting people might disagree. There might be wit. Repartee. It would happen by the picture lights and candlelight, and the light and the conversation would spill out through the windows past the lilacs, over the yard, and into the rushing creek.

Well, Mrs. Z, see what you did for that little girl who came and went from your studio? Thank you.

FOURTEEN

Raising Nora's Flag

When we bought the farm in 1988, I had never lived in the country and certainly never owned a barn. We moved in on a bright autumn day, and quite suddenly my view from the kitchen encompassed two silos and a gas pump, a large population of blue jays, and six acres of grass and creeping Charlie. There was space for our children and room for my husband to yell at his dogs with impunity.

There was also a flagpole. It stood in front of the house on the corner of the top of the hill, between an enormous pine and a precipitous drop-off to the driveway. The cement that anchored it had been shabbily finished off some years earlier, like so many things on the farm, with an unsquared square of little concrete bricks. The first year, I put in red petunias there and discovered there was only an inch or so of soil. They languished.

There are a lot of things to do with an old farm in the first few years, and the flagpole just stood there for quite some time, unadorned. The rope was rotted off, and although the pole had been constructed so that it could be lowered to the ground, the bolts were long rusted in place. A year went by before I went out one day and whacked the flagpole around, eased it to the ground, and restrung the rope.

It was my mother who gave us the flag, pulling it out of her big car along with other presents for the new old house. She brought a tea cart and two little chairs she'd been saving for me for years. The flag was wrapped inelegantly in a sheet of old plastic and rough-folded. "It's huge," she said. "It'll look great up there." Where had it come from? "It was Nora's."

When I was a little girl, we lived in a Chicago suburb built entirely around a series of country clubs, where the street names were golf-ish and vaguely Scottish: Brassie, Braeburn, Bunker, Caddy. The yard was long and deep and had enormous trees in front. Way in the back, where it was bushy and unkempt (there was no gardening in our family), you could duck down and then jump up on a pair of boards that crossed a little ditch that ran water in the spring. Scrambling up an incline, you emerged into the air and light and openness of the Illinois Central Railroad commuter line. There were probably six tracks, although it seemed like more, and across that forbidden expanse were the tops of houses where unfamiliar children lived. I didn't know anyone in that neighborhood.

Freight trains clanked by in endless parade, each car swaying a little differently, the couplings holding hands. At night, the *City of New Orleans* sped along, and in its downlit windows you could catch an occasional glimpse of an arm or a woman's hat. Each morning, commuter trains arrived from the south and stopped at our station. Every twelve minutes between 6 and 9 a.m., all the fathers in town got on the trains and left for the city, leaving behind a society made up entirely of women and children.

Women drove men to the station in those days. If they were late, they came fast down our street, careening toward the station, turned an impatient left to go under the viaduct, and paused to let the departing breadwinner leap out with the inevitable briefcase and newspaper. In winter the men wore topcoats. In the windows of the passing trains, standing or sitting, they all swayed in unison, absorbed in their papers, which were triple-folded in a curious commuter kind of way. No one conversed. No one looked up. So, northbound, the men probably never saw the southbound trains, heading from downtown out into the suburbs.

To meet those southbound trains at the Flossmoor station, the women in station wagons drove back, slower, and waited at the end of our street. Other women got off the trains, coming to work carrying string bags. Each one got into a station wagon and was driven away. Sometimes there were children in the back seat and sometimes not. But the women driving were always white; the women arriving were always Black. The ladies of the suburban houses were picking up the maids. Ours was Nora.

I was a child, living a small and circumscribed life. It never crossed my mind that both drivers and passengers in those station wagons were women. As I look back now through the tunnel of years and geography, I see that they probably had more in common with each other than with the heads-of-household who had departed on the earlier trains. But gender was nothing to bond over then, at least if you were female. And color was a division so deep as to be subterranean. At least if you were a child. Or at least if you were white. Or at least if you were me.

The only Black people I ever saw were the maids. There might have been an occasional handyman or gardener, but a Black man would have been a cause of uneasiness, unless deemed elderly and therefore safe. Black women were just women, of course, and just colored. It seemed natural to tell them what to do. A young housewife could do it, even a child. They appeared in the morning and disappeared at the end of the day into the viaduct and gone. I never wondered where Nora had come from or where she went.

I don't remember ever picking Nora up in our station wagon or in the big green Chrysler. She must have walked. The house wasn't far down the block, almost too close to the station for prestige, in fact, although it was large and gracious-looking.

There is much about those years that I do not remember. My father was getting worse by then and had probably begun the drug abuse that would be the proximate cause of his commitment to a hospital a few years later. Life in the house was a silent, somewhat fearful affair. And life outside the house was entirely artificial. Most emotion was simply shut down. The physical state of the house, except for the two front rooms and the foyer with the fountain, reflected the systemic and deep disorder of life there. Maybe Nora just cleaned the two front rooms. No one could have cleaned up the whole thing.

I do remember bits of Nora. The bits are only visual. I do not remember ever having a conversation with her or, indeed, speaking at all. One glimpse: she made fried chicken on Thursdays and I remember that nothing else tasted so good. The grease bubbled in the pan around the legs and breast pieces; she grinned as she poked it. Maybe she was grinning at me, the solemn child, watching. There was not a lot of grinning in that house. Maybe that's why I remember it so clearly.

In a photo of me at that age, I am wearing a white blouse and a cardigan sweater and a plaid straight skirt. Seated at the piano bench, feet reaching a bit for the pedals, concentrating on my piece, I am looking hard at the open music book on the rack in front of me. My hair is in two braids. My glasses are new. The photo helps me imagine myself, remember myself, practicing. This was the way I practiced, elbows stiff, focused entirely on the page, never looking down. No intonation at all, and no pedal.

Nora would pass in back of me while I was at the piano, as she crossed through the big room with the vaulted ceiling on her way to or from the kitchen. After a while (it might have been years), I was aware that she was watching me as she went by. She was not much taller than I was. And after a while longer, she stopped one day and came into my vision and spoke to me. She said, "I don't need no music," and made a movement toward the piano stool. I got up right away and stepped back. And she sat down.

I had seen Nora seated heavily on a kitchen chair from time to time, legs splayed out, resting, particularly after scrubbing the linoleum with the brush and pail. But I had never seen her sitting down anywhere else.

She looked up at me sideways, her dark hands poised over the keys. And she played. She didn't need music, and she watched her hands. They made music that was rollicking and full and loud and involved a lot of chords rolling way up and way down the keyboard. It had a beat and lots of pedal that made it all kind of run together, unconstrained. It was nothing at all like my teacher Mrs. Salter and her piano parties.

I don't know what Nora saw when she looked up at me from the piano and her hands. She stopped, though, and quickly. She went back to the kitchen, and I went outside to play or maybe up to my room at the far end of the house. I don't remember saying a word.

It can't have been too long after that, though, that she stopped and pulled something out of her apron pocket and gave it to me. "It's a jaw harp," she said. When I didn't react, she said "mouth harp", and stuck the little thing in her mouth. It and she began to make a strange, twangy sound. I remember looking at the skin under her fingernails, which seemed very pink against the black.

She handed the strange thing to me, and it was cool and a little damp. It lay in my little-girl nightstand drawer for years. It never crossed my mind to put it in my mouth. It never occurred to me to try. I felt nothing about it.

My mother, who was not interested in memory, told me that Nora was about the same age as my grandmother. She had a son who was "not quite right," whom she supported by doing housework, going to a different house every day of the week. The son was, for a time, a kind of janitor in one of several buildings my father owned on Chicago's South Side. The buildings, I was told, had "gone Black." Later on, all the buildings were condemned. My mother said Nora brought her the flag on one of her train trips to the suburbs. My mother supposed there was no place to display it in an apartment building.

The flag is a casket flag, given to Nora at the death of her husband, who was in the service in World War II. My mother did not think he died in the war, but she did not really know. The flag is big enough to have been laid on a coffin and covered it, to have been folded in that triangular fold and handed to the widow. It is muslin and well-made and soft with age; the white stripes are cream-colored. The fabric on some stripes has worn quite away.

In the last stages of illness at home before my father signed himself into a mental hospital and never came out, he cut off all the household cash, including the $10 or so a week that had gone to Nora to keep those front rooms picked up. She was elderly by then and very stiff and slow. According to my mother, she didn't do much actual cleaning. In the front rooms, she polished the surfaces. And she still made chicken as she had for fifteen years, every Thursday.

I doubt that Nora's separation from my family was done kindly or with any grace. Little was, in those days. My father shuffled around the house in his bathrobe, raging and then begging for pills. My older brother had gone off to college, safely away and distant. In high school then, I have no memory of a goodbye to Nora or of much else. I also do not remember the day of my father's commitment to the hospital, just a few weeks before I left for college and my own life, where I would trade in my lime-green matching pantsuit for wide-legged jeans worn ragged on the bottom and where, for four years, I would watch protests go by but never join them.

Nora probably just got on the train one day for the last time and rode it back north into the city, disappearing into the life we'd never imagined. I doubt that anyone in our house gave it a thought.

I don't know when Nora died or how, or what became of her son. It was years before my hard-earned armor, pierced by the birth of my own children, permitted me to remember much about being the little girl with the braids at the piano or what happened over time in the big house with the backyard near the trains. In those years, I learned to sing, and forgot how, and remembered again. I continued to play piano as long as someone told me to, then stopped, and then began again. I worked in the musical theater, and it was that passionate work that finally taught me that music made me happy. I learned to listen, and at my best, I learned to let music wash through my heart and come back out again, carrying along pieces of my lost and forgotten feelings.

And I learned to open my eyes and see what was around me, women and men, friends and allies. I learned to see human connection, that synaptic splash of recognition and reciprocity, a kind of brief coupling and communion. It is a series of these splashes, these moments, these people, that illuminate our time as we travel from darkness to darkness.

I never thought of Nora during those years after she was gone, but kindness does not go away forever. Even the smallest acts, like a moment at a piano or the gift of a jaw harp, reverberate in a child's deepest mind and are saved and remembered. Although I did not see them then, I now recognize the gleam of joy in Nora's music and the touch of pity in her eye for the little girl and her sequential piano music books. The bond is partly one of gender; after all this time, I recognize the warm woman's breeze of understanding. The mother in me now, remembering, thanks Nora for her kindness to a little girl who was learning to play the piano without feeling a thing.

I like to think that Nora could tell that I had music inside me, carefully contained somewhere behind my new glasses and above my tight braids. She saw what I could not, being blank and blind to her, as I was blank and blind to so much outside and inside the doors of that difficult house.

On holidays, my children and I get out the old flag. They argue sometimes over who gets to fasten it to the rope with clips; Maggie's little hands are hardly big enough. My husband pulls the rope slowly. We hold hands and sing "The Star-Spangled Banner" as Nora's flag rises toward the blue sky over our farm. The kids sing the parts about the bombs bursting and the rockets; my husband hums along and smiles. I throw my shoulders back and belt it out, standing with my family on the edge of the hill by the big pine tree in Minnesota. We have to start low at the beginning to be able to reach the high part at the end, and sometimes we just start over and over. Five hundred miles and decades away from the past, we raise Nora's flag and sing.

PART THREE

Noticing the Good World in Travel

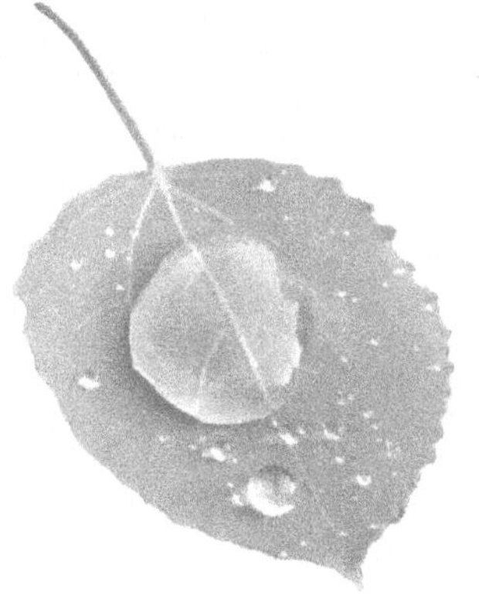

FIFTEEN

Meeting Harriet

Those who read history are blessed or cursed with double vision. We see the present as normal people do, but we also glimpse, in ghostly overlay, the shades of the sepia past. Unscarred land, settlements and villages, canoes and bateaux and steamboats and levees drift and drape over the present landscape. Sometimes we can see, and sometimes hear, people moving over the land, exploring, setting cornerstones, living out their lives in the populated past.

And sometimes, when we keep our eyes open to the doubling and stop to read the small signage of the world, those distant dead, animated by our notice, can reach out from the past into the present, tap us on the shoulder, and lead us back into their lives.

That's what Harriet did for me.

I nearly ruined my legs and knees and lungs one summer day climbing a bluff above a river town in Iowa. I'd chosen the area for its serenity, but for me as for most people, the ideal of quiet is nearly always tempered by the need to be available. So, after arriving and settling in and admiring the wide curve of the Mississippi, with the town of Lansing on its edge, the bluffs towering above and the eagles (or perhaps they were turkey vultures) higher still, I dutifully opened my cell phone only to discover an unanticipated kinship with my historical predecessors. I was, as they had been, completely out of touch with anyone outside my immediate field of vision. No signal. And no backup. The shell of a pay phone still stood down by the ball field, but only ragged wires remained.

There's one sure place to go for good information in a small town, and that is the public library, where the sympathetic ladies had a single suggestion for me. Go to the top of Mount Hosmer, to the city park, up near the turkey vultures, in order to . . . what? To be closer to the cell phone satellite? To establish line of sight with my home phone in distant Minnesota? Someone, at some time, they thought, had gotten a signal up there. I should try.

It was a warm afternoon with a high, cloudless blue sky. I had a water bottle, was lightly dressed, and needed the exercise.

It took me one hour and fifteen minutes of constant climbing to reach the top of Mount Hosmer on a closely curving paved road, pitched like Stair-Master. On my left, boulders and dense woods reaching toward the sky. On my right, a fall would lead to certain impalement on the town's steeples. The warm afternoon turned into a hot afternoon, or perhaps I was growing closer to the sun's corona. No one drove by; I would have dropped on my knees and begged for a lift.

When the narrow road finally flattened and opened out into a wide park with tall trees and hummingbirds, I rested, panting, on a stone wall, looking down on the town and the distant roof of the public library. I saw two tiny figures come out the back door, tip their heads back, shade their eyes, and point upward in my direction. I waved.

I *could* see Minnesota, I thought. And a wide sweep of Wisconsin and the place where more rivers joined the labyrinthine Mississippi and its broad braid of wetlands and water and woods. A turkey vulture flew by, below me. The cell phone didn't work.

I walked through the park, which was deserted. There was a veterans memorial and a playground. There were picnic benches. And there was a small, blue metal sign, put up by the Iowa sesquicentennial commission, long enough ago for the bolts to rust a bit. I stopped to read it, and here is what the sign said—and this is how people who love history end up getting lost in their research—*Mount Hosmer City Park was named after Harriet*

Hosmer, a noted sculptress, who won a foot race to the summit during a steam-boat layover in 1851.

I stood there, sweating and still breathing hard, and read it again. A sculptress. Ran a footrace. During a steamboat layover in 1851.

In 1851, upper-class women were wearing six or perhaps eight heavy petticoats under dresses with long, dragging skirts and tight sleeves. Propriety called for an unnaturally narrow waist, bound by tightly laced corsets stiffened with whalebone or steel. Women of that period commonly relied on banisters to climb stairs; servants had to carry the lamp and the children. The sculptress had run a footrace?

In the next few months, I spent some time reading up on Harriet Hosmer. She was twenty-one in 1851, the daughter of a liberal Unitarian family in Watertown, Massachusetts. She was said to be athletic. Some sources said she'd been raised by her father as a boy, after the deaths from tuberculosis of her mother and a sibling.

Hosmer was midway through a highly adventurous steamboat journey, first from St. Louis to New Orleans and back, and then aboard a "floating palace" called *The Senator* going from St. Louis all the way upriver to St. Paul. She was traveling with a female companion and no chaperone, a highly unusual state of affairs. The trip was paid for by an indulgent and wealthy mentor, who later became the president of Washington University in St. Louis. The contemporary material referred to this journey as her travels "in the Western Wilderness." *The Senator* had pulled in at Lansing to let off a passenger for Galena, Illinois, and to take on wood to feed its boilers. Miss Hosmer came out on deck to admire the scenery and then asked Captain Oren Smith if she would have time to climb to the top of the bluff. An unnamed gentleman offered to escort her. Smiling, she challenged him to a footrace.

The story was collected some ninety years later from a woman who claimed to have been a witness and must have been a child at the time.

They started up the bluff. She was soon far in advance of her escort. She went up toward an opening in the cliff, veered around the protruding rocks at the end of the cliff, then, striking the old Indian trail that followed the brow of the bluff, soon gained the summit. While her valiant squire was pantingly trying to catch up, Miss Hosmer stood waving her handkerchief at the stewardess who, standing on the guard of the boat, was frantically ringing the breakfast bell and shaking her turbaned head. Miss Hosmer met her companion on the way down.

The defeated gentleman suggested to two local worthies breakfasting with the captain that the bluff be named after her, and Harriet Hosmer "graciously accepted," reported the witness. "She was very pleasing in manner and appearance, rather tall and slender. She appeared to have a remarkable personality," the witness wrote, recalling her childhood conversation with Miss Hosmer: "She talked to me about the wildflowers and the birds, and asked me many questions. She noticed some wild strawberries growing nearby."

After her journeys in the western wilderness, Miss Hosmer did become a noted sculptor, and rather a scandal. In that following year, she decamped from Boston to Rome, making sculptures and selling them and living an unfettered life. She became part of a circle of intellectuals and hobnobbed with literary figures such as Robert and Elizabeth Barrett Browning and Nathaniel Hawthorne. Her personality was no longer reported as "remarkable." Now it was called "abrupt." She was known for her eccentric, practical style, her man-tailored jackets, and her short hair.

And perhaps my favorite detail, she was reported to have been working on the invention of a perpetual motion machine before her death in 1908.

Since my long climb up Mount Hosmer, I have grown very fond of Harriet in the way a person can become fond of the historical dead. You're interested in the events of their lives. You seize on any surviving glimpse of personality. You make a timeline, just to be sure you notice the amount of time they spent studying in Europe and the various ages they were when they touched the public record or made a certain splash somewhere. You read up on steamboats and artists and women of the period. You think about the sources of artistic inspiration and how they surface in a body of work. In wondering about how one climbs a bluff in a whalebone corset, you read about clothing of the period and about the beginnings of women's dress reform. You note that in June 1851 an East Coast ladies magazine printed a fashion plate of a new kind of ladies garment, quite revolutionary. Bloomers were a variation on Turkish pantaloons, covered by a skirt to the knees with a loose tunic above. The operative word here is *pantaloon.* They were *pants.*

People who love history are always reassembling the world from disparate details. With no one to contradict you, you are free to imagine that athletic Harriet—the young, female artist from a prosperous liberal family, raised to be opinionated—saw the plate in *Godey's Lady's Book* and had her seamstress go to work.

You fill in the blanks, you allow the overlay, until one dreamy day at your desk, you see the steamboat, its fires banked, laid up at the levee in wild Iowa. Third-class passengers are trudging back and forth carrying wood to the boilers. The captain is breakfasting on the top deck with businessmen who are laying out a town. Playing on the bank is a small girl with an observant eye and a good memory. A young woman with a long and lively life ahead of her steps out of her cabin into the sun and shades her eyes to look up at the high bluff and what might be an eagle. There is banter between her and a gentleman, and a challenge. She retires briefly to her cabin and appears again, in bloomers. Sensation! And up the bluff she goes.

I was back in Lansing this year. I stopped at the library and bought some books from the sale table. I ran into a fellow who told me that he'd once had to call out the volunteer fire department to rescue two people who'd tried to descend the Mount Hosmer bluff without using the road.

I drove to the blufftop and stayed a long time, thinking about Harriet and her footrace and watching the Mississippi curl north and south to the horizon. I'd found one of her sculptures at the Art Institute of Chicago and two more at the Smithsonian American Art Museum in Washington, D.C., and I had stood a long while in those places too, trying to see through the marble to the ghost of her hands and chisel.

In Chicago, her sculpture in serene white marble is a bust of Zenobia, Queen of Palmyra, a warrior queen who led a famous revolt against the Roman Empire. Nathaniel Hawthorne, I read, had written a novel featuring an exotic character named Zenobia. His novel was published just a few years earlier than the sculpture was created. The sculpture is inscribed on the back *fecit Romae*, meaning "made in Rome," where the young sculptor was acquainted with Hawthorne.

At the Smithsonian, two Hosmers similar in size and spirit flank a hallway. One of them is a likeness of the sprite Puck, round and naughty, seated on a broad mushroom with what might be oak leaves scattered below. Hosmer carved it in 1856, five years after racing to the summit and then, triumphant, asking a little girl about the local flowers and birds. Puck's hallway companion is a will-o'-the-wisp of the same period. Near his plump toes, a turtle peers out from some aquatic vegetation. I like to think that mushrooms, layered leaves, and perhaps a turtle entered the mind of the young sculptor on the banks of the Mississippi River in Lansing, Iowa, on the day she ran the footrace in her scandalous bloomers.

SIXTEEN

Work of Beauty on a Gray Day

The upper floors of the Palmer House in Chicago are so confusing that one sees other guests, rolling bags in tow, get off the elevator, and stand puzzled in front of little signs with arrows, then wander haplessly off, past portraits of all the famous performers who played its Empire Room in its heyday. Turn left at Judy Garland, bear right at Louis Armstrong, left again at Liberace. If it's January, the streets below will be cold and gray and cavernous.

In my eighth-floor room, I dropped my bags, making a pile of my coat, vest, hat, gloves, and boots. Pulling up the window shades, peering right and left, I glimpsed the L train at one end of the block and State Street at the other, and then looked directly across at the flat face of a former department store and into something entirely unexpected.

A long row of enormous plate-glass windows revealed well-lit rooms full of broad worktables, cabinets, clothes racks, and dress forms against every wall. Young intent workers were bent over their close work, cutting fabric, draping, pinning, stitching.

Investigation was in order; I hit the sidewalk. Behind a street-level security door, two blank-faced uniforms heard my inquiry about the workers, but the woman behind the table lit up. "Are you looking at the seventh floor up there? Those are the kids from the Institute," she said and smiled. "Aren't they just something?"

The School of the Art Institute of Chicago has a Fashion Design degree. Fashion is theory, fashion is history, fashion is the future, and in the case of these young artisans, fashion is making.

At the old Guthrie Theater, I used to walk through the costume shop every day, smiling and nodding, not disturbing its air of enclosure, concentration, and skill. Opening night was always approaching; and the drapers, the stitchers, the first hands, and the wonderfully imperial costume director all had a lot of work to do. These Chicago workrooms had that same air. A design assignment due, perhaps a runway show? They seemed to be on deadline, and deadlines can be the very anatomy of creativity. As Samuel Johnson said in 1777, in quite another context, "Depend upon it, sir, when a man knows he is to be hanged, it concentrates his mind wonderfully." The students were concentrating.

On Thursday and Friday of my visit, the rooms were active whenever I looked. On Saturday, they started the day dark. But as I was packing, I looked out and saw a young Black man with an upright hairdo flip on the lights and put an enormous cloud of white tulle on the table. He fluffed the fabric, tossing it into the air and letting it drift. He circled it, regarding. He sat on a nearby table, swinging his legs, looking at it while swigging from a can of something. He approached it and tossed some smaller pieces into the air. He glanced at an empty dress form at the end of the table, then rough-folded one bolt and shook out another length along the big table, watching it. Getting friendly with the fabric.

I turned away and, when I looked back, he'd added a portion of something slinky and gold and metallic to the table, and a helping of what might have been a cream-colored charmeuse. He held some tulle to the dress form at the shoulder, figuring out the shape of his intention, before figuring out the structure. Once he had the structure, he would build it all, from nothing but bolts of fabric and an idea.

I couldn't see the young man's face, but I could see his hands moving over the material, touching it lightly. Making something from nothing in the old department store room on a Saturday city morning, which was gray-skied and damp. Alone in a long row of empty workrooms, he was tossing the fabric and letting it settle and seeing something beautiful. Lit up by his idea.

When I left, in a cold rain, the bellman put me in a cab saying, "Come back. It's better in April." He did not know that up on the seventh floor across the street, the lights were on, tulle was drifting, and it was already something very like spring.

Atomic Las Vegas

I was flummoxed by Las Vegas last year on my first visit there. Feathered showgirls on the street for photo ops, along with Midnight and Rhinestone Cowboys, and the occasional dominatrix brandishing a plastic whip. The Neon Museum, fiery and glowing in the night. The shuttle driver Eva Las Vegas, who makes a stop at a liquor store, and the Italian American Club, where everyone looked like an extra from *The Sopranos*. Wedding chapels. The Garage Mahal. The Liberace Mansion. *Flummoxed* might not be the right word. Bemused, confounded, a bit overwhelmed? And a touch of charmed.

The city caught and surprised me repeatedly. Once it was a woman insistently calling me on the street to enter a spa to have my feet nibbled by goldfish. A private home cryogenic chamber on display with a rack of promotional material. One cryonics magazine in a display case had a headline story called "Culture Shock: Thinking about Re-integration after Preservation." First sentence: "A common concern expressed by individuals contemplating cryopreservation is the possible difficulty in psychological adjustment to an unknowable future." Well, yes, now that I think of it, I suppose that would take some pondering.

Travel is so broadening.

The image still on my mind from Vegas, though, is a sculpture in the lobby of the National Atomic Testing Museum. The statue is called Miss Atomic Bomb.

In the 1950s, as international rivalries and the Cold War drove expansion of our country's atomic capability, the federal government poured money and programs into the desert outside Las Vegas. A bare sixty-five miles from the city, bombs were exploded at the Nevada Testing Site. The formerly sleepy city grew 161 percent in ten years. Along with gambling and the Strip, the city sprouted an atomic tourism industry. Blast watch parties were held on hotel roofs. In early 1952, live-television coverage began, and atomic fever swept the country. Popular new designs of almost everything went atomic: atomic cocktails, dish patterns, cereal boxes, and toys, including a home laboratory containing an actual piece of uranium to make the little Geiger counter click. The box said U-238. Hope no children ingested it.

Later that spring, something arrived that seemed truly Las Vegas, a kind of unholy marriage between tourism and showgirl-ism and the Cold War. Small-town newspapers carried a photo of an atomic pinup girl—Miss Atomic Blast. Showgirl and dancer Candyce King was anointed after a watch picnic at the Last Frontier Hotel. A photo caption said that she "radiated loveliness instead of deadly atomic particles" and "dazzled US Marines who participated in recent atomic maneuvers." They found her "as awe-inspiring in another way, as was the 'Big Bang.'"

In the following years, Ms. King was succeeded by three other atomic pinups who won beauty contests and rode in parades. The photos were widely distributed as part of the culture and allure of Las Vegas.

The statue of Miss Atomic Bomb that stopped me in my tracks in the museum lobby has a horrifying look, or perhaps a horrifying resonance. Her arms are flung up, her chin lifted, her knees cocked in a showgirl post, her body clad in a mushroom cloud; is she smiling or screaming? The nuclear test ban treaty, I read, was signed in 1963 after eight years of negotiations; work must have begun on the ban as the Atomic pinup girls were being distributed and touted.

The treaty and fear held the threat of nuclear warfare in some abeyance, but in January 2023, the metaphorical Doomsday Clock was moved very close to midnight. Headlines were dire. April 3, the United Nations published on its website this article: "Many Speakers Voice Concern Over Increase in

Dangerous Nuclear Weapons Rhetoric Amidst Ongoing War Against Ukraine."

In May 2023, leaders of the G7, an informal bloc of industrialized nations, which includes the United States, Canada, France, Germany, Italy, Japan, and the United Kingdom, held their summit in the Japanese city of Hiroshima, the first place in the world to suffer a nuclear attack. The American bombing on August 6, 1945, killed an estimated 140,000 people. The survivors, called *hibakusha*, did not know if the G7 leaders would hear their message.

The former leader of the museum at the Hiroshima Peace Park said the exhibits could not possibly tell the whole story, since they can reproduce sights and sounds but not smells. "The smell that 140,000 citizens emit when their bodies rot and are thrown under the blazing sun cannot be forgotten, even almost 80 years later," said Hiroshi Harada, who was six years old and a mile away from the blast center in 1945. He survived because he happened to be standing in the shadow of the train station. His family was trying to leave the city.

The G7 leaders wrote messages in the guestbooks at the museum during their visit. Harada described the messages as "superficial." I suppose there were photo ops.

Perhaps the Atomic Testing Museum is less dusty and more relevant than it first appears. Perhaps bemused is the wrong response to Miss Atomic Bomb. The museum is Smithsonian-related now, and tour guides are drawn from former workers at the test sites. Our guide, a retired testing engineer, wore his identification badge from 1984, his younger face fresher than the one he now wears, although both were smiling. When he worked the underground tests, he said, it was 1,200 feet down to his workplace. When our group stepped into the faux bunker at the Ground Zero Theater, the simulated explosion shook and rumbled as he told us not to worry about the flash. We'd be fine, he said.

We would definitely not be fine. No one would be fine. Take a close look at Miss Atomic Bomb. The Doomsday Clock is now set at ninety seconds to midnight.

EIGHTEEN

National Bundt Day

Essayists can, occasionally, be confessional, so brace yourselves, readers. I have a problem with bundt pans. Visit the factory outlet store and you may develop one too.

In the years of dedicated home-based volunteerism, there are many situations in which one brings food to a gathering. Committee meetings, celebratory gatherings, teacher gifts, children's parties. Graduations, memorials, retirements. Welcome to the team. Farewell and best wishes.

Parent groups can be particularly pernicious, since there is often someone who bakes or cooks competitively, living for the moment of reveal, sweeping the cover off an elaborate creation from a home-based test kitchen, smiling modestly at the cooing of observers, with ears sharply pricked for attention.

(I admit that these solitary-in-preparation volunteer efforts were infinitely preferable to group decision-making. I remember spending thirty minutes early on in a group of women trying to hang a banner in a school auditorium. Should be higher. Lower. It's not centered on the wall. It's crooked. Could it be less wrinkled? "Oh," I remember exclaiming, "look at the time!")

My defense was the bundt cake. My secret weapon was and is a fancy pan. Yes, these are military and strategic terms, a touch hawkish, even a trifle martial. My arsenal fills a good-sized kitchen table.

In a fancy bundt pan, the most pedestrian of cakes shines . . . absolutely presides . . . over the buffet. After all, as Julia Child said, "a party without cake is really just a meeting." Thousands of recipe options range from the simple (a tricked-out cake mix) to the elaborate (studded with treats, festooned, elaborately layered, and frosted on the horizontal, flowers peeking from the center hole).

On the flavor, well, suit yourself. Phyllis Diller noted, "I like to serve chocolate cake, because it doesn't show the dirt."

November 15 is National Bundt Day. The idea of the bundt started in Minnesota through a small family company that later became Nordic Ware. In 1950 the company was asked to develop a pan reminiscent of Old World gugelhupf pans, which were cast iron, heavy and largely for fruitcake. The pans were sold for a fundraiser by a Hadassah, a Jewish women's organization. The fundraiser was a success, but afterward the pan didn't sell much; production was nearly discontinued. Then in 1966, a woman named Ella Helfrich took second prize in the famous and popular Pillsbury Bake-Off. Her entry: a cake called Tunnel of Fudge, baked in a Nordic Ware bundt pan. The resulting publicity led 200,000 people to write Pillsbury and ask where they could find a bundt pan. Nordic Ware eventually made 30,000 pans a day, and the bundt surpassed the tin Jell-O mold as the most-sold pan in the United States. By 2016, Nordic Ware had sold more than 70 million bundt pans across North America. A number of the originals are in the collection at the Smithsonian.

One can learn about National Bundt Day from an abundance of websites that identify every day in the year as an opportunity for promotion of one thing or another. No day is untouched! Some of these websites appear to be substantive. Some appear to be translated from a language so alien as to be extraterrestrial.

"National Bundt Day is celebrated every year all over the country with a view to spreading the joy of bundt cake that is one of the favorite foods for citizens of all ages in the United States." (Okay.)

"National Bundt Day brings happiness to all to have the bundt cake surely on the list of the food menu." (Starting to wander.)

"Every year in the month of November, this day is celebrated with a great enthusiast." (Does one advertise for this person?)

"National Bundt Day is observed not only in some of the popular cities but also in all of the places in the United States." (So, unpopular ones too.) "Many of you search for the best National Bundt Day wishes." (We do?) "By wishing them using these, you can make them surprised." (Uh . . .)

So, in the spirit of surprise, I wish you a happy National Bundt Day with this sentiment via, apparently, an alien intelligence: "When it's National Bundt Day, look nowhere and enjoy the day very much!" And this inspiring idea, from someone named Unknown: "I love to have a bundt cake, not a bread cake. Bread cakes are too mainstream and monotonous."

Finally, this stirring observation: "Snake people know how to make a bundt cake."

Let's just leave it there. Happy National Bundt Day to all!

NINETEEN

A New York State of Mind

I was head over heels happy in New York City earlier this year, happy to a ridiculous degree. The city always feels right to me, more alive than anywhere else, with its avenues and languages and crowds and glimpses of sky and constant changes and trees planted on rooftops and precious green spaces. Everything you need is within fifteen minutes. New York City is young, always young. It vibrates. *Sassy* seems like a diminutive word, *brash* is overused, *bustle* is too small-scale, *cocky* too full of subtext. Language, in this case, might be insufficient.

Although it is prudent to be prudent in the city, it never seems hostile. Coming down from the Edge, the 101-story-high super-tall outdoor sky deck, dizzy from the height, I asked a sharp-looking young man to interpret his T-shirt graphic: F$Sheart.

"The first word," he said slowly, "is the vulgar one. Then money, then S for *spread*, then heart for *love*."

"Then it means," said I, "f*** money, spread love?" He looked a little shocked to hear me say that, and then smiled a *yes*.

(Another favorite T-shirt, in a very different key, spotted on a paunchy gentleman: Sorry, Girls, I Only Date Models. Close second: You Don't Win Friends With Salad.)

I was on an urban geography adventure. Five Days, Five Boroughs. "I've never been in the Bronx!" I'd said to my husband. "I've never been to Queens!" The tour was all walking and public transportation, led by an NYC historian named John Kriskiewicz.

True enthusiasm is a fiery and contagious engine, and John is deep-hearted and enthralled by his city. He threw off facts, opinions, and *bon mots* in an enchanting stream. "In New York," he said repeatedly, "everyone is a critic." So we all became critics, enchanted critics.

Here's a list of things I learned:

- 24 million people live within a hundred miles of the Statue of Liberty.
- About the loss of old Penn Station and dissatisfaction with its replacement, the architectural historian Vincent Scully said, "Through Pennsylvania Station, one entered the city like a god. Now one scuttles in like a rat."
- When the new Moynihan Train Hall was a post office distribution center, that's where volunteers came to answer all letters addressed to Santa Claus.
- Languages and slang overlap in New York. One can, and does, "schlep to the bodega." And an idiot, whether barreling heedless down the sidewalk or driving through a crosswalk full of pedestrians, is called a "chooch" from *ciuccio*, southern Italian slang for donkey. A random group of adults deployed the new word with impunity, exclaiming, "What a chooch!" with frequency, disdain, and laughter.
- On Staten Island, a different guide—highly opinionated, verbal, and married to an Italian cop—remarked that the island has less crime because, in order to escape, the criminals would have to stand in line and wait for the ferry.
- There is a secret, unmarked bar frequented by actors and theater folk in the district, up a flight of stairs right next to a really famous place. It has a name but no signage and no street number. No, I will not tell you where it is.
- In the Bronx the Andrew Freedman House for Indigent Millionaires is endowed as an old-age home for millionaires who have lost their money. It is an NYC designated landmark.

- On Arthur Avenue in the Bronx's Little Italy, you can wander along a street of delis with a dizzying array of olive oils and restaurants owned by five generations of Italians. You can also visit Madonia Bakery to buy a box of cannoli and watch them filled to order behind the counter.
- Also in the Bronx, there is a bewildering, crowded, wonderful deli, where it's best to just say, "Give me something good for lunch." The deli is next to a place giving samples of their own wine in plastic cups.

I texted my Midwest husband: "I'm moving to the Bronx." He promptly replied, "I'm really going to miss you."

From 1937 to 1954, a radio program called *Grand Central Station* ran on the major networks. The series had a wonderful opening narrative with a dramatic voice and an echo sound effect:

"As a bullet seeks its target, shining rails in every part of our great country are aimed at Grand Central Station, heart of the nation's greatest city. Drawn by the magnetic force of the fantastic metropolis, day and night great trains rush toward the Hudson River, sweep down its eastern bank for 140 miles, flash briefly by the long red row of tenement houses south of 125th Street, dive with a roar into the two-and-one-half-mile tunnel which burrows beneath the glitter and swank of Park Avenue, and then . . . (sound effect: a train pulling into the station) . . . Grand Central Station! Crossroads of a million private lives! Gigantic stage on which are played a thousand dramas daily!"

That is exactly the way I feel about New York City.

And one last thought. It is best to simply embrace a certain amount of disorientation in New York City. Everybody does.

From the top of the Edge, eleven hundred feet above the street, the wind howls around the plexiglass walls, and you can see the full spread of archipelago Manhattan framed by saltwater. From there, our guide John attempted to orient us by pointing out the Empire State Building and the Chrysler Building with its distinctive art-deco tower. I nodded and then looked away and then looked back but couldn't find the tower. Yes, reader, I lost the Chrysler Building in the canyons of Manhattan.

I was in a New York state of mind.

TWENTY

Miss Valentine at the Circus

The light is dim and uncertain. Beside the runway, on a flight of high steps, sits an old woman with a beautiful face and an astounding sequined hat. Beyond and all around, a sea of rapt faces stretches up and away, turned toward the central brilliance like a field of flowers turns to sunlight. Scattered through the crowd are balloon sellers and ice cream men and men carrying poles dangling cones of cotton candy. The hawkers' hats have long black tassels and gold letters that spell, mysteriously, *Zuhrah*. Children in the audience wave light swords, à la *Star Wars*; many wear electric headbands that blink colors in the dark. There is an audible crunching in the air; the kids are chewing as if they've just discovered food.

Behind the bandstand, muscular men in exotic outfits are warming up with handsprings and cartwheels. One, a little older than the others, grins and waves at a little girl sitting sideways in her mother's lap. Mom is watching the ring; daughter is watching the acrobats. The girl lifts her hand solemnly, safe in the height of the bleachers. "Hello," she says in a small voice.

Tethered to the wall are five horses: three brawny and honey-colored, a spotty-rumped Appaloosa, and a shaggy white pony with a painted circle around one eye. A handcart stands at the ready, heaped with a rainbow of sequined costumes. A big sombrero moves of its own accord. Turns out, there's a poodle underneath it. There are quite a few poodles back there animating clothes.

From above comes the blare of hard-driving band music with plenty of percussion and a hot first trumpet. The music ends with a flourish. The ringmaster calls boomingly to the crowd, urging the children to let the performers know that an audience awaits. The response is piercingly treble, louder and louder as the ringmaster implores again and yet again. A lion coughs and speaks, and the roar is taken up by five other lions. Showgirls line up; small boys, and larger ones too, whoop as they think they must. A moment's heady pause, and the showgirls plunge from the dark into the light. Framed by the bandstand, brilliant with color, filling three rings with Amazing Activity, Ferocious Felines, and Lovely Ladies; this is the 66th Annual Zuhrah Shrine Circus.

Freeze it.

Take away light swords and battery-powered headbands. Move the scene, intact, from the Minneapolis Auditorium to 1908 and "the new armory building on Kenwood Boulevard." There the crowd was witnessing a brand-new phenomenon: an indoor circus.

"In Europe," the *Minneapolis Journal* informed readers, "the indoor circus is really the thing. . . . Arrangements for lighting the Armory brilliantly by electricity were made this week." The spectacle at hand was the Rhoda Royal Indoor Circus, "a travelling organization that has been appearing in a number of the large eastern cities." In fact, Rhoda Royal Indoor Circus had appeared just a few miles to the east in St. Paul, to a record-breaking attendance of 40,000.

General admission cost fifty cents; reserved seats in the balcony cost an extra quarter, or two bits. Box seats were one dollar. Each day the papers published the names of the box-seat purchasers for that evening's performance. One writer called the indoor circus "a more elaborate affair than the public understands or the Shriners themselves had counted on."

In 1908, the circus added a special attraction in the Cities: Oklahoma Bill's Cheyenne Frontier Wild West Show. Oklahoma Bill presided over "wild western sports" and, for the finale, the lynching of a horse thief. During Monday's opening-night opening number, a bucking bronco leaped the railing and tore into the crowd. The bronco-busting portion of the program was canceled. On Wednesday, a happy replacement was found: a free exhibition of bronco busting outside the Armory on the Parade Grounds, thirty minutes before the main show. Fifty dollars was offered to anyone bold enough, brave enough, and skillful enough to ride High Tower, the bronco who had created such a sensation on opening night. One wonders what the Shriners must have thought as High Tower vaulted the railing, scattering Minneapolitans like so many sparrows.

During the Circus Week of 1984, Shriners' red fezzes bobbed everywhere through the crowd at the Minneapolis Auditorium. Men's organizations can sometimes seem faintly sinister, with their lodges and funny hats and secret rites, but it was difficult to imagine a cheerier, more pleasant group of people than these Shriners. Each Shriner, whether selling peanuts or directing people to their seats, seemed to be having a genuinely good time; some took a Circus Week vacation every year and hadn't missed a performance in two decades.

In the dark confusion during "The Star-Spangled Banner," I watched one Shriner escort a small child in the wake of a woman with a baby. The woman turned to him. "Excuse me, but I think you have the wrong child," she said. "That one's not mine." The Shriner stopped, smiled, and herded his stray back in the direction from which they'd come. If he was groaning, it was inaudible.

The Shrine clowns, the Funsters, were much in evidence, having and making a good time. They warmed up the crowd, mingled with the kids, signed programs. They were also in the show in two elaborate routines featuring complicated props and dialogue with Colonel Lucky Larabee, ringmaster and straight man. The clowns talked to everybody. I saw a huddle group practicing to sign "hello" to deaf children. "They loved it! They just went nuts!" one Funster said later.

The sheer carefree fun of it all was justified, as if justification were needed, by the knowledge that the Shrine Circus was a fundraiser, a distant relative of the bake sale. Shrine circuses from coast to coast support a network of Shriners hospitals and burn centers for children, where small patients can be treated free of charge. The Zuhrah Shriners estimated that the 1984 Circus Week in Minneapolis would net something like $200,000 for kids in need—which just made the whole affair seem still more festive.

Royal Hanneford Circus prop men, performers, and producers dash from one task to the next, sometimes changing clothes en route. Describing her work, a tall blonde woman said, "Well, I was hired as a clown, but then they found out I could sew, so I'm the wardrobe mistress now. I make half the wardrobe. And I'm a showgirl in the second half. I ride the elephants. I do production too. I'll only be here 'til Wednesday, because then I have to go meet up with our second unit." With that, she rushed away to help with an elephant's birthday party.

Ina the elephant was turning fifteen. She had a cake. Her larger associate, Tina, helped her eat it. One of the elephant handlers, a thin man with glasses, anxiously questioned the Shriners and the publicity people: "There's no plastic or rubber in there? Nothing an elephant couldn't digest?"

During the show, the handler moved elephant props into and out of the ring at great speed, tapping insistently on one huge knee of a mammoth subordinate who relinquished a tub-top stance too slowly. Before and after each show, he supervised elephant rides, lifting children (mostly) into Tina's elaborate howdah and cautioning them to hold on. The girl helping the small elephant riders back down the steps was one of the equestriennes, minus spangles.

Few in the audience took notice of the restless metamorphoses all about them, as performers shed one spectacular skin in favor of another. It would have taken a keen eye to appreciate that the man who introduced the ringmaster in a red jacket and ruffles was also the man who appeared soon afterward, bare chested in tights, as the Artistic Aerial Astonishment, and who still later galloped past you in brilliant orange and feathers during the equestrian act, and who finally stood before you as an elephant handler. Your program listed this man as Superintendent of Properties.

On Wednesday, the wardrobe mistress/showgirl/clown went on to the second unit as promised, leaving a vacancy in the "Sequined and Spangled Spectacular: Journey With the Entire Cast of the Performers and Animals to a Childhood Land of Dreams and Experience Our All New Living Fairy Tale—Circus Holidays." The February holiday spot for Miss Valentine stood empty. Producer Tommy Hanneford, a resourceful fellow, saw me standing, taking notes, and smiling. He asked me if maybe I would like to go Out There. "Out There?" I said, stupidly. Hanneford gestured expansively toward the ring and, upon my astonished nod, collared a passing equilibrist.

"Put her in the Valentine costume," he said, "and get her Out There."

"Come with me," said Miss Kim, "and hurry."

Miss Kim and I disappeared behind curtains. In the dressing room, long tables were covered with makeup and paraphernalia. Costume racks bulged with splendidly bright clothes—some voluminous and others minimal, to say the least. If you have the body of an aerialist, you don't need much in the way of adornment. I was relieved to be handed a costume of the voluminous sort—entirely sequins and Velcro with billowy sleeves and a hoop skirt spangled with hearts. It was red, decidedly red. Miss Kim, looking dubious, tossed me a sequined strip. "Do something with your hair," she said.

At the other end of the table, the lion tamer's wife was changing clothes and telling about a time when the cats got away "and ran right up the aisles."

A pretty woman with thick false eyelashes donned a pink cap to match the electric-pink leg wraps on her horse. "I think I will wear the pink today," she said and grinned. A young woman with a petulant face talked about her horse's work at the afternoon matinee. "God, he was a brat," she sighed.

I got out of my jeans and boots and into my costume. I struggled with my hair. "Does this happen often," I asked, "that some strange woman comes in here and gets into a costume?"

"All the time," said the woman in pink.

An old woman, very old, came into the dressing room and began to change, slowly, into a long, gold-sequined gown. Then she put on a large, fuzzy, blue bathrobe. Mrs. Hanneford, the producer's mother, was ninety-five years old and traveling with the show. She came from "an old vaudeville family," and she looked wonderful in sequins.

Miss Kim, who had done a whole act while I was getting half ready, came back in for another change. She grabbed a red-and-white flower from a table. "Try putting that in your hair," she said and was gone.

A small boy walked up to me, now bedecked in red sequins and holding a notebook. He looked up. I waited. "Becky wears that costume," he said accusingly, then turned and walked away.

The time had come for my Sequined-and-Spangled circuit of the ring, and I took my place in line. I tried to strut. I managed to avoid falling over my hoop skirt, and there were no cries of "Fake!" or "Becky wears that costume!" If Colonel Larabee was astonished to see an unknown Miss

Valentine parading toward him, he didn't show it. And the follow spots did not falter when they found me and focused on my bright sequins.

"Miss Valentine!" the colonel boomed, and I tried a pose.

Then my moment was over.

The policemen backstage, also Shriners, rewarded my performance with grins and hugs. "We've been working this show for years," one said, "and we've never gotten Out There." They went looking for a camera. I said that I felt fortunate that none was handy. But no one (not even I) believed it. I was a little slow getting back into my jeans.

The circus has a backstage as well as its show-off side. It is close and purposeful behind the bandstand. Everyone knows precisely what needs to be done. It's like an actor's green room, where energy seems half suspended. While the Funsters are Out There exploding an outhouse that turns out to be a phone booth, the equestrian act is starting to assemble—the riders in orange and sequins. The women carry spears with feathers drooping down and lean them against the bandstand while making last-minute adjustments to their hair and body stockings. They are lithe and strong-looking, with makeup heavy enough to withstand the ring's intense lights. The horse trainer (who is also the elephant trainer) is in a blue, skin-tight, and faintly iridescent costume. His fancy jacket conceals a secret stash of carrots.

The big horses are held by the bridles before going out, but they don't seem impatient. The pony walks loose, responding to a low whistle when he roams too far. He practices his tricks in the dark for a carrot reward. Walking behind his trainer, the pony scoots unexpectedly between his legs. The riders laugh a little. As the music changes, they move toward the runway and grab their spears. Hanneford takes up a whip from the prop table and moves out with them. He will handle the horses, as his family has handled them for several generations, while the riders leap and somersault. One of the prop men whispers to me that the big, gray Percheron was a farm horse. When the circus people first saw him, he was pulling a plow. The farm horse trots by, steady and massive, going to work. Hurricane Hoof Beats takes the center ring.

Public attention is a hard thing to get these days, and it has never been an easy proposition to bring a single cry of surprise or applause from six thousand people. But in a world increasingly populated with lunatic media thrills—where the flick of a switch can bring you anything from multiple car crashes to *Battle of the Network Stars*, all in full color—the circus is a comforting place, home to the fantastic but not to fantasy. The circus is unswervingly real, unmistakably not television. There is real danger and real spectacle in every act. Spectators are properly awed, properly alarmed. And if the aura of excitement dissipates fifteen or twenty rows back, well, buy your seats farther down, ringside, close enough to smell the lions and see the sweat on the aerialists. Buy popcorn. Applaud wildly. Then savor the moment when all danger is past, when the performers return in their capes and costumes for the Fantastic Flag-Waving Finale.

Mrs. Hanneford, blue robe discarded, is escorted to the center ring like a queen. The follow spots strike fire from her gold sequins. When the ringmaster introduces her, she smiles brilliantly and casts off 50 years. Flags fall from the rigging over all three rings. The ringmaster takes off his hat. The band pauses. In the audience, a Zuhrah clown lifts a child high to see the moment. "God bless America!" Colonel Larabee cries. "And Mrs. Hanneford!"

TWENTY-ONE

Bienvenidos a San Miguel de Allende, Mexico

I returned this year to a place I'd never been.

San Miguel de Allende is a city both magnificent and somber, full of high-altitude light and bad air caught between the mountains, garlanded doors and secret patios with fountains and tile and flowers, where the sound of the street becomes indiscernible. Two thousand doors, and two thousand courtyards and *callejones* laid out for burros and carts with small taxis and small vehicles squeezing through.

In March when I went, absolutely everyone, including dogs and wildlife, moved into the slightest shade in midday, and absolutely everyone came out after dark in the mild air. The near-full moon and two aligned planets hung above the pink-faced parish church *La Parroquia de San Miguel Arcángel*, and many other churches where statues styled with agonized faces stood still in the night. Outside of town, *la luna* rested in the notch of the deserted pyramid *Cañada de la Virgen*. Having seen the moon resting there in a space that Meso-American astronomers built for it, stone by stone, around two thousand years ago, I will always see it there.

I carry vistas and landscapes in my thoughts from the state of Guanajuato, but for me the churches and architecture and landscape and artwork are largely secondary. For this particular traveler, it is ever and always the people. Encounters, however brief, are the thing that proves that I'm away and also the thing that proves I'm at home. Every small connection, with its dollop of serotonin, weaves the world closer together.

Glances. Brief exchanges. Friendly nods. Stepping aside for someone else, a child, an old one, *un viejo, una abuela*. A smile over a mispronounced word or resorting to hand gestures and an interrogatory eyebrow. Falling back into English and seeing the listener turn to someone else for a translation. Devolving into some kind of pan-global language of your own invention in which words or phrases are suddenly and mysteriously uttered in French. Or Italian. The instinctive, the intuitive, the unabashed, the essentially brave attempt to communicate.

One night in the *jardín*, I settled at the end of a long bench with a Mexican family, excusing myself to a woman with long hair and a good dress. She hastily moved her hat. I said, "Your hat is in no danger." And she said, "I don't understand English," in perfect English.

They were in the *jardín* for a birthday, lovely Sofia, age eighteen. They hired a large mariachi band (white clothes with *conchas* down the sides of skirt and trouser legs, a woman violinist, three men with trumpets, a big-voiced lead singer holding a big-bellied guitar). The mother pulled her daughter into the circle the mariachi band formed with the bench and began to dance. She replaced herself with a handsome boy, and the girl relaxed as they swayed and looked at each other. . . . Soon the family was all up dancing, and our group was smilingly encouraged to rise and dance. We did so, a free movement framed by the tall pink church and the welcoming gestures, under the moon, no English required. *Feliz cumpleanos, Sofia.*

In the market, an old woman gestured to us from a second-story window, above a chalkboard sign that advertised cold drinks. Up the narrow stairs we went. There was music in the café and otherwise not a soul except two possible daughters, who brought us *limonada*. The old woman danced a few steps, asked a few incomprehensible questions. I wondered if she solicited her customers one at a time, smiling and gesturing and leaning on the windowsill.

One day after the full moon, near the spring equinox and International Women's Day, *Doctora* Rossana Quiroz, whose field of study is astronomy in Meso-America, gave a distinctly female tour to our entirely womanly cohort at *Cañada de la Virgen*. The pyramid outside San Miguel was abandoned in 1040 A.D. and not rediscovered until the twentieth century.

Women were the timekeepers, she said, and therefore star-watchers. They "assigned meaning and followed objects in the sky."

Doctora taught us a special way to ascend the steep steps in silence, dusting off our energy, crisscrossing our pattern, accompanied "by all your female lineage, ancestors, and descendants." I am of Celtic descent, far away. But, ascending, I could feel them.

We visited the little museum display and looked at a photo of a female skeleton found in the pyramid and dated some 800 years earlier than it should have appeared there. "I'll point out that this body is in a womb position," she said. "This is not a death of violence." Just then, behind us, another tour group entered, led by a fellow talking about how priests at Mexican pyramids would flay human skin and sacrifice people, a bloody business. "Oooohhh," his people say. Along with *Doctora*, we moved on.

I met an American wearing the best-looking linen travel outfit I'd ever seen. Where had she bought it? "I don't remember the name of the shop," she said, "but if the van goes by it, I'll point it out." And she did, and I found my way back there for thirty minutes of indulgence.

Our guesthouse host Patrizia told her stories of the *cacomixtles* who scamper along the roof in the night to find apples and bananas. She enjoyed amazing the visitor and had written a book; apparently all expats have penned books. In her cookbook, besides the way to make *mole*, you can pick up useful colloquialisms, like *Esa mujer es una garnacha* ("That woman is lacking refinement") and *Que? Mis enchiladas no tienen queso?* ("What? My enchiladas don't have cheese?" which means "Aren't I good enough?"). I intend to learn these and casually throw them around, preferably rolling my R's, while certainly hoping that my enchiladas have cheese. Or at least *bravado*.

One night, several of us were starting the long trudge up from the plaza to our place. We knew better than to hurry in the uneven light on the cobblestones. As a marker along the way of the steep treacherous hill, we'd been using a building's tower hung with four bells. Looking up, we saw something above and behind that building, something like a tall tongue of flame in the night. Remarking and exclaiming, we climbed faster and, in the narrowing *calle*, met the San Miguel firefighters, who'd come in their tiny trucks to hose down a tall, skinny tree, sap blazing from bottom to top, and threatening to melt the nearby electrical wires. Why? How? Our Spanish was inadequate to understand, but sufficient to toss a bit of applause to the firemen as they drenched the tree, the street, and the surrounding walls. Botanical name notwithstanding, one of my companions decided to call it *el arbol del fuego*. Excellent.

After some days in San Miguel, I fell into a bit of double-focus vision, in which I saw the streets and sights of long-ago visits to other parts of Mexico. At seventeen, studying French, I somehow ended up as part of a Spanish class trip. I remember an excited sense of being in another country and opening the drapes in the Mexico City hotel room to reveal a building sign that was in another language. Thrilled, I rushed to the Spanish teacher, asking what "*Piernas Artificiales*" meant. We were staying across an alley from an artificial leg factory.

I brought my mother a souvenir from that trip—a carved, rose-encrusted Madonna, which is on my bookshelf now—and one for me: a small, silver, turquoise-studded crucifix. I no longer venerate either Madonnas or crucifixes, but I do honor the objects.

I carry, too, an image of myself as a Midwesterner on spring break, snorkeling off Cozumel, and stopping in fascination, hovering at the surface to watch a school of small, bright fish being moved by the water against a rough cliff, rhythmically, ceaselessly, in perfect suspension and completely invisible to the world above, with its bar patio and margaritas. I hope the descendants of those fish are still there, still schooling, still synchronized, sunlit at the top and disappearing into deep blue below.

On my last day in San Miguel de Allende, I received a great compliment. I was sprawled with my shopping on some rough steps in the shade of the artisan market, the *Mercado de Artesanías*, in my undeniably Mexican pants. I was offered a seat on a nearby bench by an *hombre* who looked, and looked again and said, "*Señora*, do you live here?"

An observant fellow. Apparently, in a certain way, I do.

TWENTY-TWO

The Flight Tracker, Over the Atlantic and Africa

Travel makes one modest.
You see what a tiny place you occupy in the world.
—Gustave Flaubert

Early this year, bound for Africa, I flew Minneapolis to Amsterdam, nine hours in an aisle seat, chosen in a vain attempt to claim a bit more legroom. Blocked from a window view, I passed time with the flight tracker, following our northward flight path across Canada. After clipping the edge of Hudson Bay, we flew eastward over northern Quebec and then Newfoundland. Occasional place names appeared on my little seatback screen and fell steadily behind.

When the continent was behind us, the tracker image over the ocean looked like a complex cloud system, grays and whites, heavily textured. And then the screen was studded with words again, these entirely unknown. I started taking quick snaps of the place names. Gloria Ridge? Imarssuak Seachannel? Reykjanes Ridge? To the south, out there somewhere in the dark, the Corner Seamounts? What on earth is the Great Meteor Tablemount?

I had always thought the ocean featureless. It turns out that the Atlantic is full of mountain ranges and ridges and plains and trenches and volcanoes which might or might not be extinct. Mountains with peaks still far below the surface of the sea. There's complex geology down there, and layering and movement of all that water.

In the dark, we were overflying a geography as complicated as the continent we'd left. Rocky Mountains? Great Plains? Consider the Mid-Atlantic Ridge, part of the longest mountain range in the world, a thousand underwater miles that divide the ocean north/south. The deepest spot in the Atlantic, I read, is the Puerto Rico Trench, at about 5.3 miles. The plane was flying at a slightly greater distance above the top of the water.

Perception need not stop at the surface; try to throw your imagination all the way to the bottom. The flight tracker and its cartoon airplane image on a road of arrows leading east gave glimpses of an entire world below. Terra entirely incognita.

Nearly three weeks later, leaving Dar es Salaam in Tanzania, I was slumped in an aisle seat again, exhausted and overwhelmed by East Africa. Flying over land this time, back toward Amsterdam, a different set of names flitted by on my seatback flight tracker. These place names, too, had been mysterious and exotic, but now? Familiar. Terra no longer incognita, but a landscape dotted with vivid images, somehow coming into tighter focus as I flew away and cast my mind down to the ground and the continent rolled by.

Right down there was Arusha, where I walked into a village and tried my first words in Swahili. *Jambo, mtoto!* I said. Hello, children! And *kwaheri,* goodbye.

Lake Eyasi, where we walked out into the bush with the Hadzabe hunter-gatherers, who laughed merrily as they roasted an arrow-shot songbird over a dung fire, offering a slice to nibble.

Karatu has a fine hospital, to which women from different tribes walk for days in order to receive prenatal care and give birth. There is a grassy lawn where they lie down and wait together.

Ngorongoro Crater, where we entered an intact and inactive volcano sheltering a simply incomprehensible number of animals. In the caldera, eighty-three threatened black rhinoceros live with their twenty-one babies born in the last three years. They are down there somewhere in the dark landscape as we fly overhead.

The plane flew over the Oldupai Gorge, called the cradle of humankind for its discoverable traces of early hominids. The more common name Olduvai is a misnomer. Oldupai is correct to the people who live there. One asked us to be ambassadors for the correct name. We can do that.

Serengeti Plains. In the Masai language, *Serengeti* means "place with no end." The balloon pilot, pointing out its vast interlocking web of animal trails, told us visitors that the Serengeti is bigger than Belgium. Somewhere below is the Masai village, the *boma,* we'd visited. In my bag is the Masai bead necklace I bought there from a woman who lifted her eyes, smiled a little, and then made us part of a line of dancing women.

Also down there are the guides, companions who became friends during our weeks together in Tanzania. The travel was rigorous and full of change, but we learned to say *pole-pole,* slowly-slowly, and to ease up, appreciating each revelation as it appeared.

Storks in a massive baobab tree. Forty-one elephants in family groups moving slowly across the landscape. A pride of lions with eleven cubs, one buried to the shoulders chewing the inside of a buffalo carcass. A herd of plumed ostriches, heads to the ground like enormous chickens. A pool full of hippos. Stately giraffes, in a kind of slow motion. A thousand wildebeest crossing the road, knobby-legged babies racing to outpace their mothers. Each creature going about its business in serenity and equanimity, unperturbed by observation, and watching for predators.

Before my journey, I thought of Africa as an immense blank canvas. It is still immense but no longer blank. Flying over it now, I can feel its abundance; it is teeming, studded with a string of images, my own memories, like little pieces of light in the dark.

Noticing the Good World in Nature

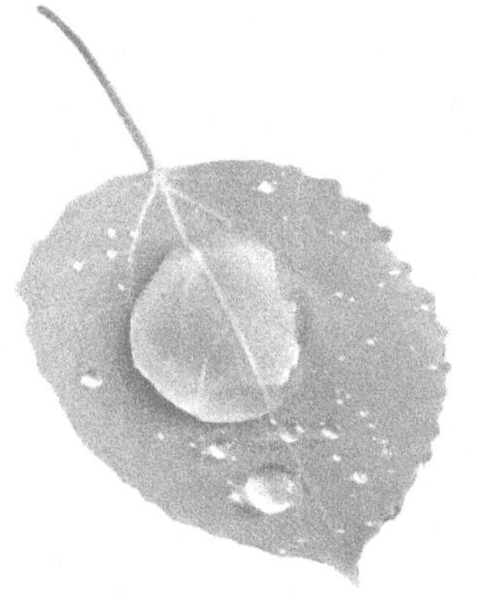

TWENTY-THREE

Skyway Flowers

I live on the skyways of St. Paul, Minnesota, an above-the-street series of enclosed walkways, a habitat which runs through buildings, jumps airily across the city streets, and permits a certain separation from weather. Last week we had a cold snap, with a blustery wind channeled between the buildings, making little snow clouds skitter along. I was crossing the bridge between two industrially brown buildings when two women appeared ahead, in winter drab, chatting amiably and pulling two carts behind them, full of miracles, astonishing to the eye. Garden carts crowded with pots of semi-tropical plants in pink and orange and yellow and deep glossy green. Kalanchoe and cyclamen to replenish the planters at one of the downtown banks. I stopped them to exclaim, although my real purpose was to extend my pleasure at this reminder of another climate, another season, and the vivid colors so absent in our northern winter landscape. The colors poured into my eyes. Then the carts rolled on and so, refreshed, did I.

The massed colors (of Widow's Thrill, Fantastic Flaming Katie, and others) have been diminished since, confined in stainless-steel planters in groups of three or four among patches of plastic grass against interior hallways and the cold marble walls of the bank. Passing, I stop at the planters and, glancing over my shoulder, finger my way past the leaves and push a finger deep into the wet soil. It smells like spring.

TWENTY-FOUR

Peonies

The house I grew up in had an enormous peony garden in the back, several hundred square feet, in an actual square, crowded with rows of plants that once a year burst into a field of color and fragrance. Pink, white, deep red, singles, doubles. My mother used that as the occasion for her peony party, which was some version of what she imagined as an elegant garden party, well-dressed people holding drinking glasses, making Good Conversation, in a sunny light.

The garden had come with the house, which had belonged to the school principal Mrs. Echols, who must have hybridized all those peonies. I wonder if it was hard for her to let that glorious garden go. My parents bought it in 1951. About the first thing tiny Peg did there was fall down the long back stairs into the basement, then attend Easter service in the new parish with white gloves and two black eyes.

The flowers are one of my earliest memories. I suppose my parents must have hired a gardener to maintain the peonies and keep the garden reasonably orderly, at least for some years. The peonies fell out of my active consciousness as a young teen, becoming not particularly noticeable, just part of the atmosphere. That's about the time the in-house atmosphere became darker, or maybe I got big enough to understand that other people's houses did not include rage.

In any event, the garden eventually decayed from neglect, and the peony parties ceased. All parties ceased, I think. My mother could not maintain a proper public shine on the household as my father declined into drug use and mental illness.

I'm not sure I can write about that glorious garden without writing about the decay of the household. So here I'll just say that I only know of one of those plants that survived, moved when the house was sold around 1970. My aunt did the digging and the rescuing and moving. (The example of her small, tidy life had done some rescuing of me too.) She moved it to her home in the dunes along Lake Michigan. The peony survived and put out leaves every year but never bloomed in the sandy soil.

Eventually, I dug it up from there and carried it to cold Minnesota, where it flourished in our front yard, in direct line of sight of the front door so I could glance at it every day. When we sold that house and moved into a downtown apartment, I transplanted the peony to a holding garden on our business property. Peonies are long-lived.

I've marked it closely during its bloom period, so it can be located in the fall and a portion can be moved to Milwaukee and planted in the back yard of my son's home. There, my little granddaughters will be able to marvel every year at the deep pink-purple petals and the perfect corona of yellow in each bloom. Another segment will go to my daughter's yard in a small town. Maybe this year, I'll get around to finding out its varietal name. We just call it the family peony.

Going to Aunt Janie's on the two-lane highway—called Red Arrow because of its history as a designated escape route in case the Germans invaded the Midwest during World War II—we always patronized a little springtime self-serve flower cart. It had a rack of plastic cups, each holding a nosegay of tiny irises, purple and yellow; daffodils and jonquils of various hues; and peonies. One dollar each cupful, honor system. I was in the habit of cutting a plastic soda bottle in half and carrying it in the car so I could safely transport the little blooms. Many a nosegay sat on the old family dining table in Janie's house overlooking the lake.

When Janie died near Memorial Day, I backtracked the flower cart to the inland flower farm that supplied it. I bought masses of peonies for her funeral. Afterward, we moved them to the gravesite in their variety of little vases. When they began to droop and drop, and the relatives had gone, I went to the cemetery one day, took each tiring stem in my hand, and shook the velvety petals off onto the fresh-turned earth, covering the rectangle with spent flowers. The headstone was set apart from the grave, in a line with other markers for the convenience of the lawn mowers, but I know where her actual grave is. I covered it with peonies.

TWENTY-FIVE

The Red Deuce Tomato

Midsummer last year I was traveling over to Michigan, a journey I've been making for decades. For most of that time, I used the old route, down through Chicago and around the bottom of Lake Michigan, where every interstate truck moving long-haul across America crowds the hundred miles or so of available freeway before springing free. In aggregate, I have probably spent weeks piled up in that traffic.

These days I prefer the Lake Michigan car ferries. The northernmost, the SS Badger, runs from Manitowoc, Wisconsin, to Ludington. It is a wonderfully aged coal-fired behemoth, which makes the four-hour water journey seem oceanic. Evocative, scenic, historic, and highly recommended. In due course, the shoreline appears, with its lighthouse, dunes, and vast beaches; and you are there. Somewhere entirely else.

On the Michigan side, I turned my car south and drove through resort towns. Along the way, I spotted a new-to-me roadside farm stand and stopped to buy provisions. Good cheese, artisan crackers, and whatever produce was in season.

The proprietor was a smiling, strong woman, dressed head to toe in Harley-Davidson gear. We discussed the growing season for a few minutes as I admired her stock and then asked, "I haven't been in before. What should I definitely buy?"

She paused and grinned, and I had the feeling I was undergoing some kind of evaluation. She said, "Would you like to have the best tomato you've ever had?"

I, of course, grinned back and said, "Yes, I most certainly would."

She took me into the back to stacks of carefully packed cartons of fruit. When she took a top off, I could smell their tomato-ness. Round and bright red, heavy for their size, nearly identical in shape. "They just came in today," she said. "They're grown for us by the Amish in northwest Indiana. I take all I can get from them. For the next few days, my family will only eat tomato sandwiches. Here, buy this sourdough and get some good mayonnaise; that's all you'll need."

"Have any bacon and lettuce?" I asked.

"Nope," she answered decidedly, "and you don't need them. Just these tomatoes." And what was the name of this paragon, this exemplar, this champion of tomatoes? "The Red Deuce."

I was traveling alone, and you don't put tomatoes in the refrigerator, so I bought the sourdough and the mayonnaise and just three Red Deuce. And that was dinner and that was breakfast and that was lunch, and it was the best tomato I'd ever had in a lifetime of good-tomato enthusiasm.

A week or so later, I called the stand. With ardor and in supplication, I said, "I want to pick up tomatoes to carry home, but I'm looking at your hours and you'll be closed when I'm driving up to the ferry. Here's what I'd like to do. I'd like to buy the tomatoes now. Can you put them out under a tree in your parking lot, outside your security fence, so I can pick them up after hours? Throw a sack or something over them; I'll take the chance of someone else finding them. My risk. It'd be evening when I'd be coming by."

"Nope."

"Please?"

"Look, I'm sorry. But we have cameras. If my husband sees anyone driving in and coming up to our place outside the security fence . . . well, he'll shoot you."

And that was the end of that.

I spent the rest of that summer calling around the state of Minnesota trying to find someone who sells the Red Deuce. Nope again. At the end of winter, I did find seeds. The catalog described the Red Deuce in pedestrian terms as "excellent second early variety. The determinate plants produce big yields of large to extra-large fruit that have great eye-appeal and good eating quality. The fruit are globe-shaped, uniform ripening and ripen to a deep red color." Not a word about the Michigan farm stand, the Amish, or the shotgun.

We live in a city high-rise with a south-facing balcony. In short order, we acquired an extremely large plastic pot, bought a hundred seeds, and persuaded a kind greenhouse friend to start them. In due course, I'll grab a plant for me, and one each for my daughter and my son and daughter-in-law. I'll lay in a supply of sourdough and good mayonnaise. Tomato sandwiches, here we come. Maybe just a touch of pepper.

The Red Deuce. Grow, tomato babies, grow! Here, at long long last, comes tomato season.

Noticing the Good World in History

TWENTY-SIX

Theater Stories: A Stage Full of Ghosts

Theater people, undeniable rogues and vagabonds, can be affectionate, even sentimental, about our stagehouses. These affections can be both abstract and specific. My fondness for the Elitch Theatre in Denver, Colorado, where I was once fortunate to work, is both. And it is the home of one hundred years of good theatre stories, including one involving me. And, well, William Shatner.

Ah, Elitch's! The first resident stock company west of the Mississippi. The longest continuously operating summer theater in the country. Called by Cecil B. DeMille "one of the cradles of American drama." Fourteen-hundred wooden seats (plus opera boxes!) with an oversized stagehouse enabling scene changes in the grand old style, with sets built on full-stage wagons and moved by stagehands, while scenery flew in and out from the high loft overhead. (Goodbye, street scene. Hello, interior; next is the palace ballroom!) The theater was set in the middle of a historic amusement park and carried every bit of its history in its bones.

Elitch's was managed in those years by Whitfield Connor, a handsome and gentlemanly elder actor who'd been the house leading man during the 1950s, and the radiant actress Haila Stoddard, of legendary grace and stage presence. The place was full of stories and ghosts, reflective of the crackling and preposterous life of backstage. Those stories could be poignant, hilarious, revealing, or cruel. They were passed down the decades orally in laughter and bombast and sometimes tears in dressing rooms and after-show bars. You heard them from your predecessors and passed them down to your descendants, recognizing yourself in them, demonstrating that you are just one in a long line of theater folk.

The Elitch Theatre was founded in 1890, when Denver was just over thirty years old. It was part of an industry described by scholar Garff Wilson as "... theatre which had color, vigor, variety and dimension. The theatre was prosperous, enjoying the patronage of large numbers of playgoers, every-where." Theater was, he said, "a rich and lusty creation."

Elitch's was made by passionate and unusual people. Because of their story-saving impulse, we know that founder John Elitch was a man "of Herculean proportion and prodigious muscular strength" who twice lost his earnings by investing in traveling stock companies and died young while attempting to tour. We also know that his wife, Mary, managed the park and orchards and zoo as well as the theater. She drove through the premises in a two-wheeled carriage drawn by a span of ostriches, and she presided over every performance from her box full of elegantly dressed guests. In early seasons, her offerings included six weeks of light opera with four weeks of vaudeville "wholly acceptable to women and children." She lived and died in a bungalow on the grounds.

In 1895 a twelve-year-old Douglas Fairbanks proposed to scrub the Elitch stage in exchange for a ticket to the next performance. He became a member of the company. Cecil B. DeMille played minor character roles in 1906. In that same year, Sarah Bernhardt brought the first of her farewell tours to Elitch's; her series went on until 1918. Tyrone Power and Harold Lloyd appeared on the stage, as did Antoinette Perry, for whom the Tony Awards are named.

Newspaper heiress Helen Bonfils played bits and walk-ons and, later, larger parts. Reputed to be the wealthiest woman in the West, she became an actor, remained an actor, and was a favorite with the audience, greeted with a round of applause when, over fifteen seasons, she would appear as a maid with a tea-tray or a gangster's moll or as some other character. She and her fortune saved the theater from dissolution more than once. All theaters should be so lucky.

Mickey Rooney used to rush through his matinee performances so he could hustle to the racetrack to bet on the afternoon card. "I said every word! I said every word!" he is reputed to have called out on the way to his car.

Clark Gable was refused a spot in the company because the manager thought his ears were too big. Edward G. Robinson played the house prior to his movie career, and many actors played the house after their movie careers had cooled. Much later, the prima ballerina Gelsey Kirkland graced the old stage by dancing her stunning *Giselle* with the Colorado Ballet. I was lucky to be backstage with Ms. Kirkland. As I recall, she disliked the conductor's choice of tempo.

Ghosts and traditions. Until the 1950s, the annual company photo was staged in front of the theater in strict hierarchical order: Producer and director at the center, lead actors flanking them, then the character actors, the heavy, the comics, and the juveniles—all displaying their best profile and the women their well-turned legs. The photo was taken by a panoramic scanning camera. After it started, the actor at the leading edge—often the juvenile comic or the soubrette—might run around to the other end of the line in time to be caught by the camera again, sometimes looking somewhat breathless or blurred. These company photos were arranged by the entrance, so that the audience found its seats through a cavalcade of theater history.

My stern-looking and fedora-topped predecessors were in those pictures too. I was the first female stage manager to work at Elitch's. The theater offered two-week celebrity packages by my time, with well-known actors and every other Sunday off, unheard of in summer theater. On those days, we all would drive out to the Rocky Mountains with the playing company; I have strolled through a mountain meadow with Cybill Shepherd. I heard many a joke from audience-charmer Pat O'Brien, who was then near the end of his life but as vibrant as ever.

I was unexpectedly smooched in the backstage by William Shatner, touring between the close of *Star Trek* on television and its first motion picture. *Deathtrap* was full of prop weapons. Before the first rehearsal, I trundled the prop cart back to his dressing room, thinking he'd like to familiarize himself. He looked up and said that, as Captain Kirk, he had already handled every prop weapon that could possibly exist. He was right; the crossbow and the garrote were no problem. On opening night, just before I cued the curtain up, he rushed offstage, bussed me quickly, turned on his heel and went back out. Up went the curtain; the show was on.

Over those summers, I had a fine flirtation with a bass player in one of the musicals. I developed a strong dislike for a minor television celebrity who treated everyone with disdain and presented our aged and tip-dependent wardrobe man with a pair of roller-coaster tickets for an opening night gift. I hope we mistreated that sour boy mightily for the rest of his two-week run with us.

I spent time with and learned from the theater's rank of legacy stagehands, several generations of whom knew how to handle the complexities of an old hemp house, how to manage a prop-heavy show on a turntable, and how to stay attentive during a slow summer matinee with only a few cues in the dark backstage. One of them, fearful of dozing, wired himself to a cue light so my warning would rouse him with a tingle. It didn't go well.

A frustrated producer once told the load-in crew that he didn't want to hear a touring set wouldn't fit through the dock door. "Just get it done!" he said, and the boys took out the back wall of the theater. And one legendary prop man presented a particularly cantankerous female star with a broomstick as a closing night gift. He is reputed to have said, "Here. Use this for your five o'clock ride out of town."

Elitch's was a happy house, and it had its charms and habits. An Italian restaurant stayed open for our occasional private dinner parties. I remember tables set up in the kitchen at midnight, and the owner making pasta puttanesca, which he called the whore's pasta, because it supplied lots of energy and could be prepared quickly. I think he actually said "between tricks." He plunged his bare hands into cold cans of tomatoes, broke them up over garlicky hot pasta, scattered it with torn basil, and rushed it to the table. I've never eaten like that before or since.

When Shelley Winters forgot her lines at Elitch's—the audience loved her and didn't care—she claimed to be distracted by ghosts floating overhead. Attentive audience members could glimpse them during scene changes. Old, roughly framed 3-by-4 feet headshots hung high in the dim backstage, gazing down regally at the goings-on. I like to imagine benevolence and camaraderie, but if they could speak, they might have been sniffing, "Well, I was much better in that role." That is a theatrical impulse too.

One of my favorite memories of Elitch's was its proximity to the famous-to-aficionados wooden roller-coaster called Mr. Twister. As reassurance to the patrons, a park brochure said: "As a part of Elitch's daily maintenance program, a mechanic and a carpenter walk every foot of the Mr. Twister tracks every day." I can testify. I remember coming through the quiet park mornings before it opened, and noting some carpenter clinging to the wooden structure, hammer in hand, finding any spots that had shaken loose the previous day. During our shows, when the fully loaded cars labored up the incline to start their run, every light in the theater, onstage and off, would dim momentarily as the power was drawn to the coaster. As the lights would dip, the actors would slightly increase their volume.

When the stage returned to brilliance, we working folk would listen for the distant screams, knowing that Mr. Twister was starting its downhill run, and that our play was also unfolding its inevitable way toward the curtain call and a standing ovation for the stars and the company and for us. Afterward, our audience would spill out into the warm, mile-high city night, past the roar of Mr. Twister, followed shortly by all of us, the rogues and vagabonds, the kissed and the un-kissed, at the end of our workdays, going home, ready for another show tomorrow.

TWENTY-SEVEN

Mounds and Beacon, Looking East

Our apartment faces east from downtown St. Paul, and the summer sunrise pours in, bringing a fine, long view of the Mississippi curving southward toward New Orleans. It is a landscape, a riverscape of geology and sky and history, of trains and a historic airport, of high bluffs topped by burial mounds and a lighthouse that has nothing to do with water.

By some quirky domestic geometry, an accidentally perfect relationship of bluff, apartment, and windowsill height, when I am lying in bed at night and the city has fallen dark, a distant rotating light of red and white atop the bluff appears just at my eyeline. The beam is rhythmic and steady; I look at it when I'm falling asleep. It's the Mounds Park Airway Beacon, fascinating in itself and built in a place of powerful presence.

About the blufftop land, the City of St. Paul website says:

"The Indigenous burial ground that is currently called "Indian Mounds Regional Park" has been a sacred site and place of burial for over a thousand years. It is significant to living Indigenous Peoples as a cemetery where their ancestors are buried. It is a place of reverence, remembrance, respect, and prayer. When the City of Saint Paul established a park in this location in 1892 with the purpose of protecting the historical setting and spectacular views, connections of contemporaneous Indigenous Peoples to the sacred site were not understood, considered, or valued."

It is good to read that acknowledgement in the official government language of the city. It also makes me wonder about the intersection of the ancient burial mounds with the erection in 1929 of the Beacon, right in the middle of the series of mounds perched blufftop. Wouldn't the beacon have needed an excavation? Footings? Might the digging have interfered with the cemetery? I saw nothing of this in the newspaper record of the day. The Indian Mounds Cultural Landscape Study and Messaging Plan noted the Beacon was built "on top of a mound" and some electrical lines intruded into "some of the mounds."

Between 1923 and 1933, some 600 beacons were built across this country, as an aid to early aviation pilots trying to find their day-and-night way from airport to airport by looking down at the ground as they flew. Ours marked Holman Field, the original airport for the Twin Cities. The tower is 110 feet tall, crowned by a mirror that flashes every ten seconds; it is said to be visible for forty miles. The beacon installations included huge concrete arrows set into the ground and painted bright yellow, signaling "this way" to pilots peering down in all kinds of weather and light. One such arrow, seventy feet long and pointing to Holman, is still in Cottage Grove, though its companion beacon tower was taken down in 1954.

A national flight system, and certainly night flight aspirations, were partially driven by the postal service and its airmail, which at one point used a system of bonfires to guide pilots after dark. I read of a pre-night-flight method in which the mail was carried by day in a plane landing at dusk near a railway station. The train carried it overnight to another station, where a day pilot picked it up and flew onward.

Other technologies soon superseded the usefulness of the airway beacons; ironically, radio navigation was coming in as the beacon was being built. Local historian and St. Paul East Side mainstay Steve Trimble wrote: "Air travel was starting to become important in the twenties . . . people were fascinated by the development of flight . . . according to a newspaper article, 'during the summer months large crowds of onlookers throng the bluffs overlooking the airport.'"

One notable event about the intersection of aviation and the neighborhood concerned the 1929 crash of a Northwest Airlines tri-motor passenger and mail plane. It took off from Holman Field, lost power, and came down on the bluff. The pilot died, but all seven passengers survived with injuries.

Neighbors ran to help when the plane hit the bluff and caught fire. A newspaper photo shows several hundred people viewing the wreckage.

The beacon in St. Paul is among the last of its kind. Trimble reported that the Smithsonian wanted it, but the community said no. Our Airway Beacon became a neighborhood landmark, deemed worthy of renovation and repainting in 1994, and noted by a mayoral candidate who vowed to climb it after election. For years the Beacon was at the center of an annual April Fools story in the neighborhood paper—reported as due to be replaced by a salvaged water tower, or to be topped by a forecasting weather ball found in a scrapyard. One proposal sketched enormous banners to be hung from the tower asking pilots to be quiet after 10 p.m. In 2008, the Dayton's Bluff District Forum *The Voice of the Community* (and a fine one) reported, straight-faced, that the Beacon had been accidentally sold on eBay and its new owners would be using it to project huge digital ads on bluffs and on downtown buildings.

I can testify that it is a long, uphill bike ride from downtown to the Beacon, that the shade of the park is welcome, and that burial mounds still rise solemnly over the river and the valley. Signage reminds visitors that they are in a cemetery.

Steve Trimble can be persuaded to visit and tell neighborhood stories. Eagles can sometimes be seen floating above the bluff. Off to the east and below lie the fields and runways of Holman Field where, once, pilots from Chicago landed with the mail, having used arrows and beacon towers and the winding Mississippi to find their way.

Holman Field has more than 41,000 landings and takeoffs each year. Many of the planes seem to float exactly along a twenty-eighth-floor altitude, across my east window. The field's 1939 terminal building still stands, housing a fine dining restaurant with deck tables adjoining the runway. I have happened to be there when pilots and passengers pulled up for dinner. When you leave the restaurant to descend the broad steps toward your car and look up, the Airway Beacon is above you and flashing. Imagine a throng of people up on the bluff a hundred years ago, watching the miracle of flight and the downtown airport. Measure the height of that bluff and give a thought to the night-flight pilots who followed lights from city to city, wayfinding through the twentieth-century sky. And above all, consider the burial mounds, a sacred site for thousands of years, and still so.

TWENTY-EIGHT

Yankee Horde, 1861

The proximate cause of my Civil War thinking is a *carte de visite* that emerged some years ago from a cardboard box in my grandparents' home. The small image shows an upright young man in Union Army uniform; he is resolute and bewhiskered. Three separate inscriptions are on the back of the old photo. Faint pencil reads "Grandpa VW," a name which would place the scribe somewhere in my grandmother's time. One generation later, my aunt's back-slanting script notes "Great, great, great grandpa Van Wagner to Peg." Some decades later I wrote: "George Herbert Van Wagner b. 1838." I can't believe I used ink on that ancient paper.

I've long had an inclination toward Civil War history, a rich period for generalized field research. Looking at Civil War George—so called to distinguish him from three succeeding generations of Georges—led me both back and down through time and history. Reading histories, examining family artifacts, and consulting genealogy sources eventually led me to make a research trip to his home territory in upstate New York. His life began to be revealed.

George was a cavalryman in the Third New York Volunteers. He was a farmer who likely had ridden his own horse thirteen miles to little Medina, New York, to enlist in response to a call from the New York governor for 25,000 volunteers. The photo was taken in Rochester, shortly after he mustered in August 1861. This one was probably sent to his mother

Catherine or sweetheart Mary Susan; it survived 162 years in some box or another before it came to me. The young farmer was assigned to carry regimental mail from Washington, D.C., to camp and back. From an obituary: "This was constantly on the move and each morning when he left the camp he was told where to find it on his return . . . he slept alternately in a bed in the city and on the ground in camp."

According to another soldier, "many times when he arrived in camp it was late and when it was rainy he was exposed and on one of these occasions he arrived late cold wet and there being no fire and having no change of clothing took a severe cold which settled on his lungs."

October 1861, the 3rd New York Cavalry was at the Battle of Ball's Bluff on the Potomac River, outside present-day Leesburg, Virginia. The fighting was ferocious, with George on its fringes, perhaps sleeping on the ground in the rain. Within a month, he was sent to hospital and later discharged with terrible lung problems, which would never clear. They called it phthisis then; now we would call it pulmonary tuberculosis, progressive and systemic. He drew a health-related pension for the rest of his life.

In 2022 I visited the Ball's Bluff Battlefield Regional Park for a day of events commemorating the 161st anniversary of the battle. There were interpreters, tours, a Civil War band, a cannon, and a skirmish. Re-enactors marched about in period uniform, learning how to stack their arms, camping in the chilly autumn woods in period tents behind a handmade canvas sign that said "Sons of Maryland! To Arms! Our borders are overrun by the Yankee horde. Rise up and defend your sacred rights, your homes, your mothers, wives, and sweethearts."

Civil War George served for the Union, but this battle took place in the South. He was part of "the Yankee horde."

The woods were in autumn dress and the ground covered in leaves that crunched as the re-enactors marched, sticking largely to the lanes, although their forebears had fought their way through rough terrain and up and down a bluff and across the Potomac. One soldier in blue, with authentically long hair, practiced his fife alone in a field before being joined by a drummer. It was a day worth thinking about, not least because of the deep commitment and memory of the people attending. It was a solemn matter.

I looked through the woods in the direction of Washington and thought about George somewhere in transit with his mail pouch and about soldiers from both sides facing murderous fire, to lie where they fell, awaiting the rough medicine of the day. Almost 500 were wounded.

At night perhaps forty of us returned for a cemetery ceremony. The approach was lit by 259 luminaria, one for each soldier who died at Ball's Bluff. We sat facing a ceremonial cannon, each of us provided with a sheet of paper with names of the dead. Name, hometown, age. I was given part of the 15th Massachusetts Infantry roster, almost all privates, the youngest of them just nineteen.

My list included two brothers, John and William Kidder, ages twenty-five and twenty-seven, from Walker (now Taunton), Massachusetts, outside Boston. With their company, they had splashed across the Potomac in the night toward a camp that turned out to be a row of trees; the Battle of Ball's Bluff was the result of a mistake, but fighting began anyway, and lives were lost. Perhaps their mother or sweethearts had an image to cherish and save; perhaps their descendants still have them. I'd like to think so.

We each took our paper and read aloud in turn into the quiet dark. Then each person took a last look at the battlefield, and we walked out past the guttering luminaria to our lives, leaving the dead behind.

Poet Theodore O'Hara was a lieutenant colonel in the 12th Regiment, Alabama Infantry of the Confederacy. His best-known excerpt:

> *On Fame's eternal camping-ground,*
> *Their silent tents are spread.*
> *And Glory guards, with solemn round*
> *The bivouac of the dead.*

TWENTY-NINE

Myles and Mary, 1942

I was on the phone making some travel arrangements and, by luck of the draw, ended up talking to "Andrew in New Hampshire." Very helpful, a credit to his profession, and additionally, a storyteller with a fine, engaging voice. I was considering a stay at the Hotel New Yorker, a midtown Manhattan location whose enormous, red, over-street sign serves as a navigation guide at the end of a long day. Built in 1930 with a private power plant, an underground tunnel direct to Penn Station, and even an ice rink, it's an Art Deco beauty that claims it was once the most technologically advanced hotel in the country. NBC did a broadcast live from the Terrace Room. Nikola Tesla occupied adjoining rooms. In 1948, the hotel boasted the greatest number of television sets under one roof. In 1971, Muhammad Ali recuperated there after his famous fight with Joe Frazier, just down the street at Madison Square Garden. In 2001, the hotel donated 10,000 free nights of lodging to volunteers in the aftermath of the 9/11 attacks. So, a place of public history; I could hardly wait.

And yet, history is both public and private. We need stories to help bring it into tight focus. Andrew-in-New-Hampshire had one to tell.

He thought that I'd like the hotel. "In 1942, my grandparents stayed at the Hotel New Yorker on their honeymoon; my grandmother took everything that wasn't nailed down. I have a Hotel New Yorker hanger in my closet. I have envelopes and letterhead and a tabletop ad for Benny Goodman, who was playing in the Terrace Room. I have an invitation to stop by the restaurant, signed by Jack Dempsey, who was the owner."

1942. The history timeline on the hotel's website says of that year, "Due to its proximity to Penn Station, the New Yorker hosts numerous GIs during World War II en route to the European Theater. Being a big-city, state-of-the-art hotel, the New Yorker developed its own renown among GIs, many of which [*sic*] had never lived in such luxury, much less visited New York City."

So, newlyweds Lieutenant and Mrs. Burke, Myles and Mary, traveled down from Springfield, Massachusetts, to stay in luxury for their honeymoon, amid soldiers headed overseas in the fraught months following Pearl Harbor and America's entry into the war. Did they hear Benny Goodman? Dine with Jack Dempsey? Go arm in arm to Times Square? Unknown.

New York City was gearing up in 1942. The city was full of servicemen. The Empire State Building was considered to be a possible prime target for a German air raid; on the eighty-sixth floor observatory, American Legion volunteers were looking for enemy bombers. Out on Staten Island, a spy wrote in a letter to Germany: "Still no air-raid shelters. Protection against raids completely inadequate. Complete confusion." One evening, all 1,790 air-raid wardens in one Manhattan zone were summoned to a police stationhouse for a lecture on how to use a screwdriver to turn off streetlights during an air-raid drill. U-boats were prowling America's East Coast unmolested, sinking scores of oil tankers and freighters bound for Britain; the glow from New York City's lights was silhouetting ships offshore, leaving them easy marks for those submarines. (Only two months after the Burkes' honeymoon, the citywide dimout began, all exterior lighting turned down, automobile headlights hooded. Buildings more than fifteen stories were required to veil their windows.)

When Lt. Myles shipped out in 1945, a photo was taken in his uniform and colorized for the Burkes' baby, so she would know what her father looked like. It was near the end of the war by then, and he was sent to Germany, where concentration camps were being liberated and hundreds of thousands of German soldiers were surrendering.

Lt. Myles Burke was killed in action there in 1945.

Back in Springfield, his child was two years old. She would become the mother of Andrew-in-New-Hampshire who would carry the middle name

Myles. "We were cheated," Andrew would say to his mother as an adult. "You never got to know your father. We never got to know him."

Andrew knows the importance of history. His grandfather's gold star is framed and hanging in his home, and he can pick out Myles in a photo with a hundred soldiers. Lt. Burke's many letters are being digitized at the Springfield History Museum. "It's a matter of loss," Andrew said. "If they are forgotten, they die a second time."

I thought about the lieutenant and his wife, Mary, when I stayed at the Hotel New Yorker, passing through the lobby, walking up Eighth Avenue toward the theater district, descending to the subway. It is an American story, a family story, and a wartime story. One surviving detail paints Lt. Burke as a decent officer who was kind to a trainee bullied in camp as a "sissy."

"We know what that means," Andrew told me.

"If they want to give him a hard time, Mary," Myles told his wife, "they'll have to go through me." The trainee finished the long march in full gear, with the lieutenant's encouragement. A deeply honorable legacy.

I would add that this is a love story. After Myles was killed, Andrew says, Mary never remarried. She never took off her wedding ring. She saved the paper ephemera and his letters, then her daughter saved them, and so did Andrew in turn. It is nice to know that some beloved things survive as home artifacts, along with the echo of a wartime honeymoon in a New York hotel in a time that seems nearly vanished, except for memory, carried by their child and grandchild. Andrew told me about it in a phone encounter. And now I've told you.

Decent Myles in the colorized photo. Mary who saved souvenirs from her honeymoon. History is a crowded place, isn't it?

THIRTY

Letters From a Country Gone

My grandfather Frank's letters were all written to other people and came to me a few years ago in a battered manila envelope, postmark faded to a dim-pink, barely readable "July 1978." The envelope was addressed to my aunt Jane, who lived alone in the family house on Lake Michigan.

Frank had died the year before, giving up the ghost in the night in his narrow bed by a lakeside window, always cracked open to admit the sound of the waves. I sleep in that bed sometimes now when I'm visiting the house; there is a mirror by its foot with a crucifix above it, festooned with long, dry fronds from many past Palm Sundays. Sometimes I wonder if my grandfather could see himself in the mirror as he lay there.

There are phrases that occur and recur in his letters and capitalizing that represents emphasis; in the live telling, that would have been a rap on the table or a laugh followed by a coughing spell. "In my day," he writes repeatedly. Also he writes "in that country . . ." and it is not merely an old man's locution. He means "that country" no longer exists and that day was his and the modern one was not. I remember how he closed up the ramparts of his small family's life against the 1960s and its agitations, and how he watched the grandchildren grow into lanky loungers in ragged jeans who drove too fast up the winding driveway to the lake house. We were not, I think, interested in his stories, to my shame. He writes in one letter about the four of us grandchildren, "a pretty good group, but there are times when a good clean murder might be the simplest solution."

Frank was much given to using the word *etc.* as shorthand to indicate everything his correspondents already knew about the lost geography he described. Now the correspondents are all gone and *etc.* means nothing at all.

The world of his letters, so alive in his memory and so affectionately described, is the world I hope he traveled back to as his body failed. Fort Worth, Texas, around 1900:

I was raised in the country, on a place of 185,000 acres, a band of some 600 horses and at times as many as 20,000 cattle. Of course the values were very different than today, for at that time, you could buy all the land you could see for $1.25 an acre or lease it for 6 cents an acre a year.

We used to figure it required twenty acres of grass to support an animal, but in good years, with plenty of rain and good grass, we'd increase the run. When the grass was poor we'd have to reduce the run to maybe 8 or 10,000 head.

There were four boys and we had the usual array of horses, ponies, cattle, dogs, cats, guinea pigs, prairie dogs, chickens and most anything that was "pet-table." At one time we had a cinnamon bear until it grew up and was too rough on our dogs; another time we had a pet antelope, but the game warden insisted on its release. It was said many times by friends, neighbors and the like that they could never understand how our mother lived to 76 years with the four of us. What one didn't think of, the other did.

We kids were always trying something like shoeing horses, repairing wind mills, erecting fence, building pens, etc. etc. On the place we had a complete black smith shop, plumbing shop, machine shop, carpenter shop so were prepared to repair anything from a saddle to an engine. We kids did a big business loaning tools to the Mexican freighter teams (10 to 20 animals, horses or mules, to a team) for repairing a wagon or harness and in return they would bring us pets—prairie dogs, chipmunks, lizards, horned toads, birds, chickens and the like—until the place resembled a ZOO.

As kids, my brothers and I just lived for the annual events of rodeos and circuses. In my day the name rodeo had not been invented—it was known as a "contest" and in town was usually held in a ball park, but out in the country out on the open prairie. Out there it was not impossible for a horse or steer or bull to get scot free and take off for the "woods" with somebody's rope or saddle attached. Then, much commotion ensued, as in that country to lose any of your equipment because of wild or unruly stock was the height of disgrace.

In my time all camp gear, chuck wagon, etc. were moved from pasture to pasture, or range, with mules and wagons plus camp cooks which might be black, or white, or Mexican, or Chinese, but ALWAYS MEN. The crew fed at a campfire and all slept on the ground. If a rainstorm came up there would be a mad rush to get beneath the chuck wagon as the only dry spot. One man spent his time finding and bringing in firewood. In the old days "frijole" beans were the main dish along with boiled salt pork and at supper, or in very cold weather COFFEE ROYALE (in a one gallon pot with one quart of whisky added). We went to town just two times a year, at Xmas and at election, and maybe a special trip for a circus. We were 95 miles from town, a 1 1/2 to 2 day trip. We used to move our range horses at about 5–6 miles an hour. No horses were fed grain, everything was grass fed so were "soft" and used but one day a week. Every man had seven horses in a mount—six were his working horses and one his SUNDAY HORSE, which he only used to call on his girl or go to town by.

Later, the family moved to North Fort Worth, where they lived at 1700 Grand Avenue, before many streets were laid out. The boys watched cattle drives from the roof, as the stock was driven toward the stockyards. The town was rambunctious, and his letters are filled with character sketches:

Old Mr. Craig was guard on a chain gang and when we kids would visit the camp, he would invite us to eat the beans and biscuits. He was the one armed guard who always had the worst prisoners, the ones with two picks on their legs. Then there was Andy Mansker, a little bit of a fellow but rather fearless with that big gun. He used to invite me to hold and watch his horse and buggy while he served papers or made rounds. I was with him when he shot and killed a man at the GREY MULE SALOON in downtown Fort Worth.

The jail consisted of an iron cage about 8 x 8 x 7 feet in a wooden shack with no running water nor sanitary facilities. It was located about two blocks from the school so each day, we kids would have to go by to see who was locked up, and get him or her drinking water and maybe something to eat for the night. We used to hang around the City Hall where the Police were. The Police used horses and buggies for their hurry-up calls and would always take one of us along to "hold the horse" when he jumped out and caught the culprit, or most often shot him. I recall once the Worth Hotel clerk had been held up, so I was with the Police that were first there. The officer went into the hotel, and I tied the horse, not wanting to miss a single thing. The officer asked the clerk "what did the gun look like?" and the clerk quickly answered "it looked like a sewer pipe to me!" I was thoroughly bawled out for tying up the horse and then being in the way.

Of course, every kid had his horse. In summer we could get odd jobs to earn a little money; during the school year it was hard to earn. Every house had a cow or two and they could eat a lot of hay penned up all the time, so we kids had a "route." We'd take the cows out in the morning before school and then bring them home after school. For that we charged $1 per month per cow. We could handle about 25 or 30 cows but of course we always had to have a partner—more for company than work. After the first week, the cows would be waiting at the gate to get started in the morning and at night they were anxious to get home for the milking and some solid feed. They knew the way to and from the pasture better than we kids, but we still had to go along to justify our fee.

They were rascals, those boys, no doubt. Three close in age, Frank the oldest. A trial to their mother, who seems to have handled some of the liveliest situations with a buggy whip, and to their father, superintendent for Swift and Company at the Fort Worth Stockyards. The photography of the time casts a serious air on its subjects, but it is clear that John William Condon was an imposing man. It is more difficult to tell at this remove if he was proud of his rascal boys or not. As old men themselves, the brothers referred to their father as the Old Gent or J.W. for John William. They remembered their own sobriquet, apparently in general use in Fort Worth, around the yards and beyond. They were called "those damned Condon kids." Frank wrote to his brother Tex in 1964:

Remember old Mrs. Collins? I remember that picket fence being a block long but I suppose it was only 100 or so feet. Anyway, we kids would have a slat or flat piece of wood and run alongside the fence dragging the stick along the pickets. One kid was enough but when half a dozen did it, the old girl would be out there yelling like a Comanche—the noise was terrible! She was always going to have us killed if we didn't stop bothering her!

And Tex wrote back laconically: *Yes, yes, she would rave on, referring to our ancestry.*

Frank again:

Do you remember when we got the job of churning butter and separating milk at Striplings Dairy? Of course the churn and separator were hand driven and it was essential that they be operated at a consistent speed. The deal was that we were to get 5 cents for each batch, plus milk to drink. The first few times, the milk to drink was fine, but it wasn't long until we commenced to get ideas. The main one was to drink CREAM instead of the milk. I guess old Strip noticed a fall off in cream percentage; the job played out quite suddenly.

One of my numerous summer jobs, at about age 13, was to bring horses from the Exchange Building tie racks, where all buyers, sellers, speculators, yard employees gathered while the buyers and sellers argued and traded. I took the horses to the blacksmith shop for shoeing and returned them when shod; horses always required new shoes periodically as hard roads were coming into vogue. This job was quite dull and there was a goat there that probably found time a little heavy on his hands too. He was a large Angora, just an old pet we played with at odd times. One of us conceived the idea that we should train Bill the goat, so we proceeded to train him to butt a feed bucket. We'd push it against his head and then back off a little; then when he came forward for some feed, we'd bang the bucket against his horns. It didn't take him too long to realize that feed buckets were both his friend and his enemy—his friend because they meant something to eat, and his enemy because he had to butt them in order to get the food. The net result was that all buckets were to be butted.

After this training, Bill was ready to attack any bucket. So we'd sit up in front of the shop and when some workman with a lunch bucket came along we'd simply point Bill in his direction. Before you'd know it the bucket would be sailing through the air, and sometimes the carrier, too, and we'd be busy capturing old Bill and giving apologies and also preparing for the next attack.

Bill later inherited a job as Judas goat at the slaughterhouse, but he apparently still didn't escape the attentions of the Condon boys:

I recall the time we felt poor old Bill was too warm, and should be clipped. After much wrestling with him and with hand clippers the job was finally completed, but sometime during the night poor old Bill departed this world. We suspected the cause was his embarrassment.

And there was the story of the bear and the banty chicks, which I remember hearing while turning the handle of an old ice-cream churn on

Sunday afternoons. As I recall, a good deal of chortling was involved in the telling. Frank wrote:

At about fifteen years of age, I worked a summer vacation on a ranch at Ozona, Texas [he identifies the ranch by its brand, "09"] *and for three months I earned (or at least I was paid) $60. Coming home I transferred trains at Brownwood Junction and had about a two-hour layover. In roaming around, I found a middle-sized bear chained in front of a restaurant who was quite gentle, and to whom I was attracted. To make a long story short, I ended up as owner of the bear, but minus 57 of my hard-earned dollars. When the train arrived, the conductor refused to let me on with the bear. After much imploring on my part, the conductor agreed that the bear and I could ride in the baggage car if I purchased two tickets. That ate up all my money and when we arrived at the home town, I had to send for a horse and buggy to get the bear out home. Do you know how a half- wild horse acts in the presence of a bear? At home I had to placate my father as well as all the other horses in the lot, which was no easy job.*

In time, the bear, horses and family became adjusted to one another and my trading instinct came out. I started to rent the bear on a chain to neighbor kids so they could play with him. Before long I had most of the small change in the neighborhood and was reduced to letting some kid play with the bear for whatever he wanted to trade. All kids had Banty chickens so before long I had quite a flock. That, however, didn't last too long. The Bantys ran with the regular chickens and my mother discovered the cause of the reduced-size eggs. As a result my project had to be abandoned and bear and Bantys disposed of.

But their best prank, the one Tex called *the premiere of all times*, was the night they soaped the streetcar tracks. The Northern Texas Traction streetcars had a hand brake, and for a while the brothers had a friendly relationship with Bagley the motorman, who used to let them turn the trolley at the terminus of the line and get a free ride for a block or two. That was before the event in question, involving the Condon boys, the hill on the streetcar line, and what must have been a considerable quantity of soap.

We soaped the tracks on the downhill side toward 20th Street, and when the car hit the soap, it just slid past everyone who was waiting for a ride into town. It's a wonder that the car didn't fly the track. I can see Bagley right now frantically trying to make that old hand brake hold and the harder he pulled the tighter the brakes locked; the car just gained momentum all the time. I think it slid for ten or eleven blocks! Old man Bagley carried a hog leg six-shooter as big as the side of a house. He said that no one but a GODDAMN Condon kid would do a thing like that, and that he would shoot any of us on sight. When he finally got stopped, he tried to come back up the hill to catch us but he couldn't make it. He just kept sliding back. We were long gone, high tailing it for home to make up some sort of alibi.

I was back in Fort Worth a few years ago, Tex wrote back, *and walking to the Yards. On the way I passed a barber shop and thought "Well, I think I will get shaved here." The barber was working on me; he had put a hot towel on my face when a streetcar went by. I said "I remember well when this streetcar line was established." I told him about the incident of soaping the tracks and he grabbed the towel from my face and said "Are you one of those goddamn Condon kids?"*

There is in Frankie's letters a sense of cheerful mortality, particularly in the years before his death. He refers to the future as a time "after I've gone to California," which in his dry Texas boyhood must have seemed a green and verdant wonderland. He and his brothers, he reports, "are living on borrowed time" at their ages. He mentions the Old Gent with the Big Scythe. He reports his own increasingly frequent visits to the hospital with equanimity, resilience, and humor. A plain postcard (five cents) in 1971 declares, with his caps and a center-justified title:

TWO DOWN—ONE MORE TO GO (visits to MEMORIAL HOSPITAL, St. Joseph).

Now back home again after 9 days as pneumonia patient and feeling better by the hour.

Hoping for comparable good luck on THIRD DOWN.

Education on OXYGEN, INHALATION THERAPY, ETC now practically complete, nothing more necessary or desired so hold flowers.

Before I left the family nest and flew off into the world, I remember my grandfather downstairs in the lake bedroom, hunched over the battered and antiquated typewriter, hunting and pecking and overusing the carbon ribbons, waiting to be served his lunch by the women of the house. I doubt I ever asked him what he was doing. He was writing his memories to someone I never knew, someone who saved them in a shoebox. A year after his death, the kind stranger sent them back to my aunt, and there they sat in their manila envelope for thirty years until they came to me, Frank's letters from *that country*.

THIRTY-ONE

Uncle Tex's Wedding

St. Paul Dispatch, June 19, 1919.

HORSEMAN DASHES INTO HOTEL, SEIZES BRIDEGROOM

A horseman last night spurred his steed through the door and into the lobby of the Foley Hotel, Seventh and Jackson Streets, while a reception in honor of Mr. and Mrs. John William Condon, married at the St. Paul Cathedral yesterday morning, was in progress.

The horseman headed his mount directly towards the bride. Her husband quickly stepped between them to shield her from the invader. Not to be outwitted, the lone rider caught Condon in his grasp, swung his horse about, and rider and victim disappeared though the door.

Men in the lobby rushed to prevent the abduction, but were forced to retreat by a volley of shots from more than fifty revolvers, grimly grasped by an equal number of horsemen waiting outside.

While the intruders held the would-be rescuers at a distance, Condon, despite his vehement protests, was tied securely to a hayrack. The vehicle, with its cortege of shooting, howling horsemen, started up the street, a source of wonder to pedestrians.

You can learn so much from family history. Our ancestors were not stiffly posed, elaborately hatted cardboard cutouts, no matter what the pictures look like. They were people. And some of them had adventures like my great uncle Tex Condon, abducted from his own wedding reception by shooting, howling horsemen in the streets of decorous downtown St. Paul.

The bride was a very young society girl, just graduated from convent school, whose father owned the hotel that was the site of the shenanigans. Tex was a cattleman from the South St. Paul stockyards, and it was members of their notorious booster club, Hook 'Em Cow, who rousted the 250 well-dressed guests from their civilized celebration and took their pal Tex for what the paper called a "careening ride around town."

You just have to wonder what the new in-laws were thinking as the hayrack and the horsemen disappeared down the street.

Tonight is the anniversary of my great uncle Tex's (first!) wedding, and my sister and I intend to dine in the old Livestock Exchange Building in South St. Paul, where he no doubt did business. Then we will drive up Concord Street, imagining fifty boisterous Hook 'Em Cow boys, full of purpose and mischief, trotting on a hot afternoon up toward the city, where the unsuspecting young couple was receiving in a ballroom decked with ferns and white peonies. Maybe we'll carry a peony or two ourselves in honor of Great Uncle Tex's wedding.

THIRTY-TWO

Mr. Lincoln Is Asking You a Question

Young teens are deeply skeptical about enthusiasm in adults. The more fervently an adult tries to share, the more distant the students can become. The average end-of-the-year field trip can be an extended exercise in sighs, vacant looks, and adjustments of coiffure. But not always.

Maureen Conway is an expressive and energetic woman who, along with several hardy colleagues, spent years taking seventh graders to Washington, D.C., on a spring trip. The year I traveled along as parent chaperone, the count was forty-nine students, and the first tour stop was a grassy spot on the edge of Arlington National Cemetery. Standing right there near the idling buses, Conway set about infecting the children with history.

She leaned in. They leaned in. An occasional passerby leaned in.

"We are at Arlington National Cemetery," Conway said emphatically. "This is where you learn what it means to be an American. These people fought for you. These people died for you. Think about that."

Unabashedly and with vigor, she began four days of continuous American stories. At Arlington, the tale was of how Robert E. Lee's estate was turned into a Union graveyard after he became a general for the Confederate Army of the South. The bodies of the first Union soldiers killed in the Civil War were buried in his wife's rose garden. They buried the bodies in the garden? Not a backpack rustled.

True enthusiasm is highly contagious, and needed by young people who know they are growing toward an uncertain future. Catching a bug for American history is very close to catching a bug for citizenship, and the nation's capital can be the best place to pick up a permanent infection.

So what are the ideas caught by young people traveling to Washington in any given spring, in the company of a devotee of American history?

- History can stir the heart. Actor John Wilkes Booth knew the play on stage at Ford's Theatre, so he watched for his cue and shot President Abraham Lincoln during the loudest laugh line. He then leaped from the presidential box and paused at center stage to shout, *"Sic semper tyrannis!" Thus be it always for tyrants.* As Booth galloped away on a horse that had been held by a stagehand, Lincoln had begun to die. He was carried across the street and laid in a boarding house bed.
- The past was inhabited by people just like you. Learning "courtesies" of Colonial Williamsburg, the girls were instructed to try the manners of young women of that time and look demurely downward when meeting a gentleman. The downcast eyes are for inspecting his calf, outstretched politely during his bow. If his calf is muscular, he may be wealthy enough to own a horse and might be a good catch. "Check him out, girls," urged the smiling guide. "Display your left hand so he can see you are not married."
- History is personal. The school's tour bus driver pointed to photos in a special display at Arlington's Women's Memorial. He told us his eleven-year-old nephew, round-faced in his school picture, was aboard Flight 77 and died when it crashed into the Pentagon on 9/11. He had won an academic award at his school, his uncle said; the prize was a trip to California.
- Your own families are part of history. One girl found her last name on the Vietnam Veterans Memorial wall and made a rubbing to take home. I searched the wall for the name of a young man from my hometown. In college I'd worn a POW/MIA bracelet with his name on it. My mother and the lost soldier's mother had had lunch together the previous week.

In teachers like Conway and in all adults who brave the bored demeanor of teens to reveal their passionate interests, young people see a glimpse of an adult future that includes strong interests, intellectual curiosity, and a passionate attachment to ideas. A future like that cannot possibly be dull or hopeless.

Maureen Conway taught us a special way of approaching the Lincoln Memorial. Start at the bottom of the steps in the center, she said, and don't look up while you climb. Don't look up until you get to the very top step.

When you do, Lincoln will be looking right at you. And he'll be asking you this question: *What are you going to do for this country?* Don't look for somebody else to do something. It is your job to be a citizen. That is why Lincoln is looking right at you and asking, *What are you going to do for your country?*

THIRTY-THREE

The Good World Invites You In

This book is drawn from an essay series which itself was born during pandemic times. For a while, uncertainty and darkness seemed to tilt both the world and individual sensibilities. Remembering, seeking, and then lifting up moments of beauty and goodness and joy reminded me that they still existed in that gray landscape, and that they were there for me to see and savor. Others found the series, and the list grew as readers passed them to others.

The glimpses gathered here build a solid case for wonder. The good world is not always pretty, but it's beautiful and big, bracing and bright. To pay attention is a life-saving spiritual practice, and anyone can do it.

Art, history, architecture, the natural world, and wit—all retain their beauty and strength. And the joy and intimacy of human interaction, however small or sporadic, remind us that connection and stories are what knit the world—our splendid and complex world—together, and always will.

I have learned to notice the good world, everywhere and every day. Anyone can.

Acknowledgments

One of the great pleasures of writing about so many different topics is meeting people who find large and small joys in their lives, in their work, in the world, and who want to share their stories.

Among them, for this book: Ben Owen, Kipp Kobayashi, Alan Howell, Steve Ozone. Tony Vierling. Emily White, Mary Pettis. Eric Nilsson, Abbie Betinis, Andrea Jones, Jayne Johnson. Iris Zahara. Sister Antona Ebo. Scott Mayer. John Kriskiewicz. Marianna Padilla, Doctora Rossana Quiroz, Patricia Merrill. Welcome Jerde. Christopher Kirkland. Steve Trimble. Andrew M. Zuba. Maureen Conway.

Organizations who contributed to the joy in these pages: Historic Elitch Theatre, Cloud Appreciation Society, Dark Sky Sanctuary of the Boundary Waters Canoe Area Wilderness, River Valley Antique Power Association, Friends of Ball's Bluff Battlefield.

I am fortunate in my colleagues. Kathleen Weflen. Erin Scott. Scott Edelstein. Clinton Little. Special thanks to the following manuscript readers: Chris Crowley, Sue Scott, Jack El-Hai, James P. Lenfestey, Reverend Victoria Safford.

Family, in all its forms, always seeps into the writing. Thank you, all, for resting easy there.

And deep gratitude to all the readers of my Motley Peg essay series, the best imaginable collaborators.

Peg Guilfoyle

St. Paul, Minnesota 2025

www.pegguilfoyle.com

About the Author

Peg Guilfoyle's books include *The Guthrie Theater: Images, History, and Inside Stories* (Midwest Book Award, Independent Publisher's Award), *The Basilica of Saint Mary: Voices from a Landmark*, and *Offstage Voices: Life in Twin Cities Theater*. She has written two volumes of a projected trilogy on history and genealogy, and produced history books for private and corporate clients, with numerous awards, including the Minnesota Book Award. Her arts vocabulary is extensive, her professional history wide, and her curiosity unlimited. Peg is an active volunteer and board leader, and is widely involved in citizen activism. She lives high above the Mississippi River in St. Paul, Minnesota.

Peg is the author of the wide-ranging Motley Peg essay series. Read her at www.pegguilfoyle.com.

About the Press

Sea Crow Press is committed to amplifying voices that might otherwise go unheard. In a rapidly changing world, we believe the small press plays an essential part in contemporary arts as a community forum, a cultural reservoir, and an agent of change. We are international with a focus on our New England roots. We publish creative nonfiction, literary fiction, and poetry. Our books celebrate our connection to each other and to the natural world with a focus on positive change and great storytelling. We follow a traditional publishing model to create carefully selected and edited books. In turbulent times, we focus on sharing works of beauty that chart a positive course for the future.

www.ingramcontent.com/pod-product-compliance
Lightning Source LLC
Chambersburg PA
CBHW010600310726
48969CB00009B/2513